Obstacles to
the Liberalization of
Trade in Insurance

THE TRADE POLICY RESEARCH CENTRE was established in London in 1968 to promote independent analysis and public discussion on policy issues in international economic relations. Its work has mostly focused on trade policies — broadly defined to embrace all policies, however described, that bear on the production structures of economies — and other trade-related issues. These policies, along with public finance, form the core of resource-allocation questions. How those questions are handled by governments is probably the main single influence on the wealth of nations.

The initiative in establishing the Centre came from Mr Hugh Corbet, who became the first Director, and Harry G. Johnson, who was part-time Director of Studies until he died in 1977. Among the founding members of the Centre's Advisory Board, later replaced by a Council, were Sir Roy Harrod, Professor Richard G. Lipsey, Mr W.G. Pullen (the first Chairman of the Council), Professor James E. Meade, Maxwell Stamp and Sir Eric Wyndham White.

Initially, the Centre was organized as an unincorporated association, but in 1978 it was incorporated as a company limited by guarantee. In 1990, the Centre's assets were acquired by Maxwell Stamp Plc, economics and business consultants, with a view to carrying on the work through a new, and autonomous, company limited by guarantee.

The principle function of the Centre is the sponsorship of research programmes and publications on policy problems of both national and international importance. Seminars and other meetings are also held from time to time.

Publications are presented as professionally competent studies worthy of public consideration. The interpretations and conclusions in them are those of their respective authors and do not purport to represent the views of the Centre which, having general terms of reference, does not represent on any particular issue a consensus of opinion.

TRADE POLICY RESEARCH CENTRE
2 Hat & Mitre Court
St John Street
London EC1M 4EL

Thames Essay No. 58

Obstacles to the Liberalization of Trade in Insurance

BY

Robert L. Carter

AND

Gerard M. Dickinson

 **HARVESTER WHEATSHEAF**

New York London Toronto Sydney Tokyo Singapore

——— ◊ ———

for the
TRADE POLICY RESEARCH CENTRE
London

368
C320

First published 1992 by
Harvester Wheatsheaf
66 Wood Lane End, Hemel Hempstead
Hertfordshire HP2 4RG
A division of Simon & Schuster International Group

Distributed in North America by
University of Michigan Press
839 Greene Street
PO Box #1104
Ann Arbor, MI 48106, U.S.A.

Typeset by The Right Type, Twickenham

Printed and bound in Great Britain by
Billing & Sons Ltd, Worcester

British Library Cataloguing-in-Publication Data

Carter, Robert L.
    Obstacles to the liberalization of trade in
    insurance. – (Thames essays)
    I. Title II. Dickinson, Gerard M. III. Series 368

    ISBN 0-7450-1157-8
    ISBN 0-7450-1158-6 pbk

Library of Congress Cataloging in Publication
data are available from the publisher

Contents

List of Tables

Biographical Notes

ROBERT L. CARTER, Emeritus Professor of Insurance Studies at the University of Nottingham, Norwich Union Professor of Insurance Studies 1975-90, began his career with the Norwich Union Fire Insurance Society, later becoming Assistant Insurance Manager with the Dunlop Company. Since 1963 he has also taught economics and insurance at the Brighton Polytechnic. In 1982-83 he was the C.V. Starr Visiting Professor in International Insurance at the Graduate School of International Management, Glendale, Arizona.

Professor Carter has acted as consultant to a number of companies and official bodies, and is a government nominee on the Insurance Brokers Registration Council. He is the author of a number of books, including *Theft in the Market* (1974), *Economics and Insurance* (1972 and 1979), and *Reinsurance* (1979 and 1983). He is editor of Kluwer Publishing's *Handbook of Insurance*, co-editor of their *Handbook of Risk Management*, *Personal Financial Management* and *The British Insurance Industry: a Statistical Review* and co-editor of *Personal Financial Markets* (1986).

GERARD M. DICKINSON is Professor of International Insurance and Director, Centre for Insurance and Investment, City University Business School in London. He has been a visiting Professor at the University of British Columbia in Canada and in 1893-84 the C.V. Starr Visiting Professor in International Insurance at the Graduate School of International

Management, Glendale, Arizona. Professor Dickinson is author of three books and is a regular contributor to the literature on insurance, investment and risk management. He has been a consultant to companies, governments and the European Commission on insurance and risk management issues and is a Vice Secretary General of the Geneva Association.

Preface

IN THE Uruguay Round of multilateral trade negotiations proceeding in Geneva, under the auspices of the General Agreement on Tariffs and Trade (GATT), governments have been trying to formulate a comprehensive 'framework agreement' on trade in services.

Getting multilateral negotiations under way on trade in services was a tortuous task. Initially, deliberations were begun in the early 1980s in the Organisation for Economic Cooperation and Development (OECD), where the governments of developed countries discuss economic issues of common interest. Soon after, the subject was taken up in the framework of the GATT, the instrument which governs the institutional environment of international trade among market-oriented economies.

The effort began in earnest at the GATT ministerial meeting of November 1982 on the initiative of the United States (with varying degrees of support from other developed countries), at the special GATT ministerial meeting of November 1982. The developing countries, led by Brazil and India, opposed the inclusion of trade in services in the GATT. For a while, it looked as if the effort to launch a new GATT round 'to halt and reverse protectionism', to quote the Economic Summit *communiqué* of May 1983, would founder on the disagreement over the inclusion of trade in services on the agenda of the proposed negotiations. In the end, it was agreed at Punta del Este in September 1986, where a GATT ministerial meeting launched the Uruguay Round negotiations, that trade in services would be broached in a separate negotiating group, separate from the negotiations on trade in goods. In this way the negotiations on trade in services could begin without having to be associated too closely with the GATT *per se*. After three years it looks as if governments are working their way towards a General Agreement on Trade in Services.

Pursuing an interest which dates back to the early 1970s, the Trade Policy Research Centre embarked in 1981 on a major programme of studies on restrictions on transactions in the international market for services, supervised by Brian Hindley, the Centre's Counsellor for Studies. The programme was supported by a grant from the Ford Foundation in New York, but further studies have been added with the help of smaller grants from the Rockefeller, Starr and American Express foundations, also in New York, from the German Marshall Fund in Washington and from the Nuffield, Esmée Fairbairn and Baring foundations in London.

The programme included a study on direct insurance and reinsurance, which has been carried out by Robert L. Carter, of the University of Nottingham, and Gerard M. Dickinson, of the City University, London. The study follows an earlier one they did for the Centre, *Barriers to Trade in Insurance*, published as a Thames Essay in 1979.

As usual, it has to be stressed that the views expressed in this Thames Essay do not necessarily represent those of the Trade Policy Research Centre which, having general terms of reference, does not represent a consensus of opinion on any particular issue. The purpose of the Centre is to promote independent analysis and public discussion of international economic policy issues.

HUGH CORBET

Chapter 1

Recent Developments in Trade in Insurance

SOON AFTER the end of World War II the non-Communist countries began multilateral negotiations for liberalizing international trade in goods. Paradoxically, as tariffs on goods were being reduced, many governments — particularly among the newly-emerging countries — began to raise new barriers to trade in services, which became the fastest growing sector of international trade. The early 1970s witnessed a change in attitudes and, led by the United States, Western governments began to focus on the possible liberalization of international transactions in services.

The international activities of the insurance industry fall within the scope of 'trade in services' although, as explained in Chapter 2, the foreign operations of insurance enterprises through their direct investment in branch offices, subsidiaries and associated companies need to be considered in conjunction with cross-frontier trade. Over the last 30 years, while expenditure on insurance in most countries has each year grown faster than national income, trade in insurance has become increasingly restricted. Therefore, given the attention that is now being focussed on services in the Uruguay Round negotiations under the General Agreement on Tariffs and Trade (GATT), the object of this study is to provide trade negotiators, economic commentators and the public with a better understanding of the role of the insurance industry and the case for reversing the trend of increasing restrictions on trade in insurance services. First, however, we will consider briefly the attitudes of governments to insurance trade and then attempt to define trade discrimination.

RESTRICTIONS ON INSURANCE TRADE

Attempts by governments to restrict access to their domestic markets by foreign insurers is not a new phenomenon. What has changed is the proliferation of restrictions imposed by many countries since the 1950s. Governments do differ markedly in their attitudes and policies, however, and a broad distinction can be drawn between the Communist blocs, the Third World and the industrialized countries.

Since the Soviet Government first nationalized the Russian insurance industry in 1918, Communist governments have invariably expelled foreign insurers from their markets and have given state corporations a monopoly of all domestic insurance business. The international trading activities of the corporations are still limited mainly to the purchase of reinsurance from abroad, particularly to cover the risks of losses with a high foreign-exchange content, and the acceptance of reinsurance from overseas operations. The development of East-West trade and tourism, together with the activities of Communist-bloc multinational corporations, has led though to a greater involvement in the international insurance market of the state corporations. They make arrangements for the provision of insurance for foreigners and foreign corporations as well as for the overseas operations of their own trading, transport, manufacturing and construction corporations.

For example, the Soviet state insurance corporation, Ingosstrakh, which is concerned with external risks, also has subsidiary companies operating in London, Vienna and Hamburg; these companies undertake both direct and reinsurance business. Also, the state insurance companies of Hungary, Poland, Romania and Yugoslavia have formed Bermuda-registered joint-venture companies with the American International Group to accept business on a worldwide basis. Generally, however, centrally-planned economies totally prohibit residents from insuring abroad; agreements with non-

Communist governments are limited to bilateral arrangements[1]. Following the political developments in Eastern Europe, several countries are now starting to privatise their insurance industries and allowing foreign insurers to participate.

In their desire to build up their own local insurance markets, developing countries have been particularly active in imposing restrictions on foreign insurance. Their importance, however, in relation to total world premium expenditure is very small, as shown in Table 1.1. The aggregate annual premium expenditure of many developing countries is substantially less than the annual premium income of one of the large American or European multinational insurance groups.[2] Moreover, the size of the insurance markets in many developing countries is significantly less than the premium expenditure figures recorded. This is because a significant proportion of the premium spent finds its way into international reinsurance markets due to the need to transfer the large risk concentrations associated with industrial and infrastructure development and air and sea transport. Although developing countries, as a group, account for only a small proportion of world-wide insurance spending, demand for insurance in a number of these countries is growing relatively quickly; this issue is discussed further in Appendix IV.

Amongst the industrialized countries there is a move in Western Europe to liberalize trade in insurance. The European Community now gives every Community insurer the right to establish branch offices in any member state and it is working towards the liberalization of restrictions on cross-frontier insurance business inside the Community.

Some member states, notably the United Kingdom, the Netherlands and Ireland, have traditionally pursued liberal insurance trade policies and have been successful in influencing Community policy towards liberalization. As a result of the steps taken towards harmonizing insurance supervision throughout the Community, however, it is conceivable that the regulations in these countries could become more

restrictive.[3] In France, the Federal Republic of Germany and
Italy, on the other hand, the programme for the creation of
a common market in insurance is leading to a relaxation of
trade restrictions against insurers from within the Community,
and probably from third countries too, although foreign

TABLE 1.1

Shares of World Gross Direct Premium Expenditure
(Excluding Centrally-planned Economies)
(% of total)

	Life insurance		Non-life insurance	
	1978	1988	1978	1988
	%	%	%	%
North America	40.8	31.8	53.4	50.4
Western Europe	30.3	25.2	32.8	30.0
Japan	23.7	35.9	7.4	13.2
Rest of OECD	1.7	1.7	2.1	1.8
Developing countries	3.5	5.4	4.3	4.6
Total (%)	100.0	100.0	100.0	100.0
Total ($ billion)	140.2	596.7	214.8	532.5

SOURCE: Based on data in *Sigma*.

insurers may still find themselves discriminated against in other
ways. For example, the European Court of Justice in 1983
held that by failing to grant the branches and agencies of
foreign insurance companies the same benefits of shareholders'
tax credits as those enjoyed by French-registered companies,
the French Government had failed to fulfil its obligations under
Article 52 of the European Community's Treaty of Rome.

Other industrialized countries in recent years have increased
the number of obstacles which foreign insurers have to
surmount. For example, although the United States market
is not highly protected, regulations introduced by New York
State do enable the Insurance Commissioner to exercise greater

control over surplus lines and reinsurance business placed abroad; these regulations are being adopted by other state insurance regulatory authorities.[4] The sheer size of the American market makes any restrictions imposed by the state authorities important from a world trade standpoint. Foreign insurers and reinsurers are also encountering an increasing number of problems in Australia where, for instance, government insurance offices have been established to compete with private insurers; and since 1980, insurance intermediaries have been prohibited from placing business with unauthorized insurers without the written consent of the policyholder and reinsurance cessions to non-admitted reinsurers are subject to a special withholding tax. Although Japan has recently eased some of its restrictions on the entry of foreign insurers, their market share remains low.[5]

REGULATION OF REINSURANCE TRADE

Trade in reinsurance[6] is subject to less regulation than trade in direct insurance. The greater freedom of trade in reinsurance has a long history and stems from the commercial imperative for large risk concentrations to be spread internationally. The basic need for such spreading of risk is well recognized by governments in both developed and developing countries and by international agencies such as the United Nations Conference on Trade and Development (UNCTAD). There are three other reasons why governments have granted more freedom to reinsurance transactions.

First, governments that wish to exercise control over the national insurance market have grown to recognize they can do this without prejudicing their ability to gain access to the capital and technical expertise of the international insurance market because of the existence of well-developed reinsurance markets. Second, since reinsurance represents transactions between insurance companies, the fiduciary concern of the regulatory authorities is less than for direct insurance, for insurance companies can be assumed to be better-informed consumers than the general public. Thirdly, a greater use of a reinsurance is considered, particularly in developing countries, to afford the balance-of-payments savings over trade in direct insurances, although many of these savings are in practice much less than perceived (see Chapter 4).

In many commercial situations, reinsurance and direct insurance complement each other in that they may both combine to provide adequate risk transfer capacity. But areas of competition do exist between reinsurance and direct insurance as they can be alternative ways of supplying risk protection. The substitutability of reinsurance for direct insurance has had some bearing on the growth of restrictions on the foreign supply of direct insurance. Even in countries which lack the local capital or expertise to supply domestic insurance needs, it has been possible for governments to discourage or prohibit foreign direct insurance companies, knowing that they can pursue these discriminatory policies at no great cost because of the existence of reinsurance. In economic parlance, freedom for reinsurance has in some instances afforded a second best solution. But it would be inaccurate to say that this has been the general case.

RESTRICTIONS ON INSURANCE BROKING

As will be explained in Chapter 2, insurance brokers, and particularly the major international firms, play an important role in mobilizing the underwriting capacity required for the insurance of both large and specialist risks through their knowledge of, and access to, the world's insurance and reinsurance markets. Nevertheless, in many countries restrictions are placed on their activities, particularly in relation to direct insurance in countries where the tradition of insurance broking is not well developed. Hence brokers have been restricted in the Federal Republic of Germany and certain other continental European countries. In Japan the licensing of foreign brokers to arrange the international insurance needs of Japanese corporations has also been difficult; domestic or foreign brokers are not allowed to handle insurance risks situated in Japan. Ironically, the major international insurance brokers are not inhibited in many developing countries, even where there are restrictions on foreign insurance companies. The main reason for this is that they do not pose a competitive threat to local insurers, but rather seek to assist them, even when these insurers are state-owned. They facilitate the arranging of international reinsurance, help to manage regional reinsurance pools and, in some cases, offer underwriting and management skills to local insurance companies.[7]

Some state-owned insurance and reinsurance enterprises have been set up with assistance from the major broking firms. It might be argued that partly because of the support of the major international brokers, it has been possible for governments in a number of developing countries to adopt a more protectionist attitude towards their local insurance market. There may well be some force to this argument in a number of developing countries although in most cases it is likely that governments would have pursued protectionist policies in any event. The existence of the major insurance brokers can best be seen as reducing some of the economic costs that are likely to be associated with protectionist policies, for they play an important role in product innovation and in acting as an intermediary to ensure that adequate insurance and reinsurance supply is available and suited to local insurance needs.

It is not possible within the scope of this study to examine in detail the restrictions imposed by governments on the activities of insurance brokers. In Table 1.2, however, a summary is given of the main types of restriction and their possible effects; five possible situations are set out in the table. The first three are shown as (a), (b) and (c) in the table where foreign or foreign-owned brokers are totally excluded from a country's direct insurance market, being allowed neither to establish branch offices nor locally incorporated subsidiaries, nor to supply cross-frontier services. The resulting welfare losses for local policyholders increase as the barriers to the entry of foreign direct insurers to the country's insurance market are progressively raised, as shown in situations (a),

(b) and (c). The fourth situation is where locally established brokers, including any locally established foreign brokers, are precluded from placing abroad domestic risks or providing other services to foreign insurers who wish to supply insurance across frontiers. Fifth, there is the situation where foreign brokers are precluded from placing abroad the reinsurances of local insurers.

DEFINITION OF DISCRIMINATION

It should be made clear at this point what we regard as discriminatory measures because not all impediments to services are necessarily unfair or would infringe the types of conditions that have been negotiated in relation to trade in goods. Any measures or conditions which place a foreign company at a competitive disadvantage compared with a domestic company is defined as discriminatory. Thus the scope of this study embraces not only such directly discriminatory measures as restrictions on the freedom of establishment of foreign insurers, or on the freedom of residents to place their insurances abroad, but also such factors as taxation and exchange-control regulations which, indirectly, may deter foreign insurers from trading with a country. Discrimination may arise from both government-imposed regulations (including the way such regulations are administered) and from market practices, such as local insurers excluding foreign insurers from membership of tariff and other market associations, thereby undermining their ability to compete in the market.

Measures which equally affect both domestic and foreign insurers and/or reinsurers are excluded from the scope of the study even if in practice they affect the profitability of foreign companies and, consequently, their decisions regarding trade with a country. An example of such measures is found in minimum capital requirements which apply equally to all insurers seeking establishment, including the compulsory deposit of funds in local securities. If the minimum sums required are exceptionally large, relative to the amount of business which a company expects to undertake, then it may

TABLE 1.2

Restrictions on International Trade in
Insurance-broking Services

Situation	Adverse effects
Constraints on foreign or foreign-owned brokers establishing or supplying cross-frontier services in a direct insurance market:	
(a) open to supply of insurance by foreign insurers on an establishment basis.	Local corporate buyers of insurance, including government-owned enterprises, cannot avail themselves of the in-depth expertise of the large brokers in the areas of loss prevention and risk management.
(b) open to supply of insurance by foreign insurers on a cross-frontier basis.	Local buyers are additionally deprived of the knowledge possessed by international brokers when placing their insurance abroad.
(c) closed to foreign insurers	Further isolates the market from the import of new types of insurance and other insurance knowledge from abroad.
Constraints on local brokers placing or servicing domestic risks which are insured abroad.[a]	As in 1(b); it also reduces the opportunity for local brokers to gain such knowledge, thus protecting locally established insurers from overseas competition.
Constraints on foreign reinsurance brokers supplying their services to local insurers.	Deprives local insurers of an important source of expert knowledge of planning reinsurance programmes and of placing them in the international reinsurance markets.

[a] See, for example, the position that existed in West Germany, as described in Gerritt Winter, 'After the Directive: Brokers Operating in West Germany', *Policy Holder Insurance Journal*, Stockport, 30 July 1976. This led to the Schleicher case before the European Court of Justice in 1986 — see Chapter 6.

conclude that the freezing of a disproportionate part of its capital funds is too high a price to pay for freedom to trade in that country. This would apply particularly if the investment yield on funds held or deposited locally is low compared with the returns available elsewhere. Other examples are the tax or solvency margin penalties which may make establishment less attractive for a foreign company because such penalties will limit the size of risk which a local branch or subsidiary can underwrite — perhaps by curtailing the amount of reinsurance it can arrange with its parent company.

Although such measures may not be discriminatory, they may nevertheless operate against the best interests of all parties. A number of insurers have indicated that developments of this latter kind have been more important in inducing them to withdraw from many countries than the imposition of truly discriminatory measures. In some cases their withdrawal has deprived the markets of developing countries of the capacity, expertise and technology which major multinational insurance groups possess. Developing countries have not significantly reduced their country's reliance on international insurance facilities to handle large risks, however, because insurance capacity formerly provided on a direct basis now has to be acquired through reinsurance.

The nationalization of insurance business is also outside the scope of this study. It is the prerogative of sovereign powers to organize their economies according to whatever principles they choose. Nevertheless, the prohibition of establishment for foreign insurers as a result of nationalization virtually means, as pointed out above, the exclusion of international trade in direct insurance even if no constraints are imposed on residents insuring abroad.[8] If, at the same time, a monopoly state corporation seeks establishment in the domestic markets of other countries, like the Soviet Ingosstrakh or the state-owned Indian companies, then the insurers of those countries may complain that they are being discriminated against unfairly.

Finally, there are a number of 'grey' areas where measures imposed by governments in pursuit of objectives unconnected with the protection of policyholders, local insurers or other insurance-related factors may nevertheless restrict international trade in insurance. For example, exchange controls regulating the outflow of capital usually restrict the payment abroad of premiums for life insurance. Some life insurance contracts are largely methods of saving and so have a large capital content, but others only provide protection against premature death. Because of the difficulties of framing regulations which would fairly distinguish between the two, all forms of life insurance are usually embraced by the prohibition on the remittance abroad of premiums.

The aim of the study is to identify the nature and extent of discriminatory measures imposed by both developed and developing countries on the international flow of insurance services, to analyze their effects and to make some policy recommendations. In view of their welfare implications, the study also considers measures imposed by governments, such as exchange-control regulations, which prevent or hinder their own domestic insurance companies from supplying insurance or reinsurance services abroad. The next chapter sets out briefly the nature of the insurance business and its importance in international trade. In Chapter 3, the barriers to international trade in insurance are considered; and in Chapter 4, the types of restrictions which are imposed are outlined and Chapter 5 analyzes their effects. In Chapter 6 we summarize the progress which has been made towards greater freedom in international insurance; and in Chapter 7 the European experience of liberalization in the insurance trade is examined. In the final chapter we suggest ways in which some progress may be achieved in future multilateral trade negotiations.

NOTES AND REFERENCES

1. The policies of individual countries often conflict in regard to the insurance of imports and exports. For example, if both the importer and the exporter are required to insure locally, double insurance will be effected on the same consignment. To overcome

this problem the People's Republic of China entered into an agreement with Algeria for a 50 per cent sharing of marine risks. See *Marine Cargo Insurance*, Document TD/B/C3/120 (Geneva: UNCTAD Secretariat, 1975) p. 219.

2. For example, in 1987 the worldwide premium income of the largest American companies totalled $US18,415 million for non-life (State Farm) and $15,150 million for life insurance (Prudential). The largest British companies were Royal with $6,034 million for non-life premium income and the Prudential (not connected with the American company of the same name) at $5,683 million for life premiums. This compares with the estimated premium expenditure in 1987 of some developing countries as follows:

	Non-life $USm	Life $USm
Brazil	1285	237
Indonesia	496	146
Morocco	275	66
Nigeria	182	47
Turkey	283	23
Zimbabwe	102	180

The data is taken from company accounts and from *Sigma*, 3/89, Swiss Reinsurance Group, Zurich, 1989.

3. For example, the 1979 Belgian supervisory law imposes restrictions on the insurance of Belgian risks with non-admitted insurers.

4. Surplus-lines business consists of those insurances which locally licensed insurers are not prepared to write and which are, therefore, placed with non-admitted insurers. Regulations 41 and 98 require surplus-line brokers and reinsurance brokers respectively to provide the Commissioner with additional information regarding the non-admitted companies with whom they deal.

5. It has been said that 'Japan's Ministry of Finance uses administrative practices and discretionary rules to restrict the number of entries of alien (that is, foreign) insurers'. David L. Bickelhaupt and Ran Bar-Niv, *International Insurance: Managing Risk in the World* (New York: Insurance Information Institute, 1983) p. 82.

In a comment on the minimum capital requirements for companies entering the German market, it has been observed: 'It would seem, however, to be a negligible barrier if it was not accompanied by a slow and complex licensing procedure. The costs of going through this process are substantial and they are truly sunk. Accordingly, foreign insurance companies frequently complain about the difficulties involved in᾿ entering the German market.' J. Finsinger, E. Hammond and J. Tapp, *Insurance: Competition or Regulation?* (London: Institute for Fiscal Studies, 1985) p. 55.

6. Reinsurance enables an insurer to transfer part of a risk he has insured to another insurer known as a reinsurer; see Chapter 2.

7. See *Reinsurance Security for Developing Countries*, Document TD/B/C. 3/228 (Geneva: UNCTAD Secretariat, 1989).

8. In 1976 Portugal nationalized her domestically-owned companies and left foreign-owned companies free to continue operating. It is now starting to privatise the nationalized companies.

Nature of the Insurance Business

INSURANCE is a method of spreading, over time and over a wider body of individuals and organizations, the financial losses arising from the occurrence of some types of uncertain events. The industry is comprised of:

(a) the specialist risk-bearers, known as insurers and reinsurers who are mainly companies, although Lloyd's of London still operates through individual underwriting members organized in syndicates;

(b) intermediaries, of which the most important are the full-time insurance brokers who act as agents for the buyers of insurance in the placing of their insurances; and

(c) firms providing specialist services associated with insurance, such as loss adjusters, risk management consultants and so on.

The benefit of insurance is that it enables individuals exposed to specified risks to contribute to a fund administered by an insurer from which the few who suffer a fortuitous loss can be compensated. In other words, under a contract of direct insurance, in return for the policyholder paying a premium at the inception of the insurance, the insurer promises to indemnify the latter for any financial losses sustained, or to pay an agreed sum of money, if an insured event occurs during a specified period of time.

The industry operates on the basis of the law of large numbers. If an insurance company can combine in one account a large number of similar units, independently exposed to loss, then there will be a tendency for the variation in the size of the total losses which it may incur during any one year to be smaller, relative to the amount of business transacted. Thus an insurance company can reduce the risk inherent in its operations by expanding the amount of business it transacts. Two factors can disturb that relationship. First, individual risks can vary in size from, say, a $50,000 house to a $1 billion oil rig or potential liability claim. Second, there may be an interdependence between loss exposures, such as properties located in an hurricane zone, many of which may be damaged if a severe hurricane occurs. Therefore, insurers use two devices in order to spread the risk over a larger number of insurers:

(a) through co-insurance the direct insurance may be shared amongst a number of insurers, each of whom will be directly and separately responsible for paying an agreed share of any loss to the policyholder;

(b) an insurer may buy reinsurance whereby part of the risk is transferred to a reinsurer. In return for a reinsurance premium, the reinsurer undertakes to reimburse the original insurer for all or part of the cost of any claims it may find itself liable to pay on the original direct insurance. Reinsurers in turn may also transfer a number of the risks they have accepted to other reinsurers.

In most developed countries, the majority of insured risks can be handled by domestic insurance industries, particularly if arrangements are made to mobilize the underwriting capacity of several companies through the use of co-insurance or reinsurance. The highly developed insurance industries of even the major industrial countries, however, find it necessary to spread the very large risks internationally.[1] The brokers that operate internationally play a major role in the placing of the insurances and reinsurances of large risks, especially in placing them across national frontiers.

Lloyd's underwriting syndicates are entirely dependent on authorized brokers for the marketing of their insurances and reinsurances in Britain and overseas. In countries that permit residents to insure abroad, brokers provide the means of access to international insurance markets for clients who may not be able to obtain locally the extent of coverage, capacity or expertise they require. Elsewhere international brokers assist local insurers, including the state insurance corporations of developing and Communist bloc countries, in devising appropriate reinsurance programmes and in spreading risks worldwide through the international insurance markets. As countries have increased the restrictions placed on foreign direct insurers, the role of brokers in mobilizing the underwriting capacity required by indigeneous insurers and in keeping them informed of developments in insurance practice has grown in importance. Therefore it has become increasingly important that, subject to adequate fiduciary controls, international brokers should be free to operate across national frontiers.

INTERNATIONAL INSURANCE TRANSACTIONS

The international spreading of large risks through insurance can be achieved in a number of ways. First, it may take place at the direct insurance stage, possibly through the participation of foreign insurers as co-insurers alongside domestic companies. Second, domestic insurers may transfer a part of the risks they insure to foreign reinsurers. In both cases, the foreign insurer/reinsurer may operate through a local establishment; that is, an insurer/reinsurer may appoint agents abroad with binding powers to underwrite business on its behalf or it may establish its own branch offices or subsidiary companies abroad (hereafter referred to as establishment business). Alternatively, insurers and reinsurers may export insurance services in the sense that they underwrite, usually at their head offices, the insurance of risks located in other countries. Such services may be provided either for their own nationals, whether resident at home or abroad, or for foreign nationals. Hereafter this category of business is referred to as cross-frontier business, a term which is more descriptive and less confusing than the designation 'services business' as used by the European Community. We use the term cross-frontier, although the term cross-border would have been equally appropriate.

When compared with the production of physical goods, establishment business is more akin to the business of multinational enterprises than conventional international trade. For insurance companies that wish to transact a substantial volume of foreign direct-insurance business, a local establishment is generally preferred to operating a cross-frontier business, for a number of reasons.

First, unless a local presence is maintained it is difficult to have a precise knowledge of the risks involved and market practices. Most classes of non-life insurance require considerable on-the-spot pre-sales and post-sales servicing: sometimes the insurer needs to survey the risk proposed for insurance prior to acceptance or during the life of the insurance and it may be required to provide advice on loss prevention. Moreover, in order to provide a satisfactory service to policyholders, it will need adequate facilities to investigate and settle claims. In an increasingly complex world, local establishment provides an insurer with first-hand knowledge of local economic, technological, social and legal conditions required by an underwriter to assess accurately the risks which he is offered.

Second, it is generally agreed that, particularly in relation to personal insurances, individuals often need to be persuaded to buy insurance so that an insurer needs local marketing facilities.

Third, as well as providing services for local residents, an overseas office can offer servicing facilities for the company's own national policyholders who are travelling or trading or have insured assets abroad.[2]

The grounds for establishment depend partly on whether alternative marketing and servicing facilities are available locally and partly on the type of business the insurer wishes to transact. In countries where brokers, including possibly local offices of international brokers, handle a substantial proportion of the total market business and there are reliable independent firms of loss adjusters, a foreign insurer may be able to negotiate adequate marketing, surveying and claims-servicing arrangements without being established itself.

Nevertheless, if a foreign insurance company is to attract the support of brokers, it must be able to offer something more than locally established insurers provide, such as a willingness to write business that the latter will not or cannot accept, greater flexibility in premium rating or coverage or simply higher commission rates to compensate the broker for the higher costs he may incur.

As to the type of business an insurer wishes to transact, a distinction must be drawn between the needs and attitudes of corporate as compared with personal buyers of insurance. Large corporations normally possess detailed knowledge of insurance markets and practice and often need overseas servicing of their insurances. They will be less reluctant than individuals to place their insurance with non-established foreign insurers and, indeed, may prefer to deal with a major international insurer. Individual buyers, on the other hand, tend to prefer insurers with local offices capable of providing the sort of service they require and with assets maintained locally to guarantee the payment of claims.

Consequently, the larger the volume of direct business a foreign insurer hopes to write and the greater the emphasis on personal and small commercial lines, the stronger are the incentives for it to establish a local office or to appoint a local agent with binding authority to write business on its behalf. In this way, a foreign insurer will be able to provide the services required to compete against local insurers.

The apparent success of the Lloyd's syndicates does not invalidate this argument. They are able to obtain their business from the network of Lloyd's brokers, many of whom are established or otherwise represented in the countries concerned and Lloyd's underwriters have a worldwide reputation for their enterprising, innovative approach to underwriting. Nevertheless, most of their overseas direct insurance business is limited to large, specialist and/or unusual risks which brokers (with experience of, and access to, international insurance markets) cannot satisfactorily place locally because of capacity or other problems. Moreover, although Lloyd's business (as measured by calendar-year accounting premiums) has increased four-fold between 1972 and 1987 from £928.3 million to £4,194 million of which over 70 per cent is overseas business, its share of total world non-life premiums has declined.

One of the difficulties that Lloyd's and other international insurers have encountered is that, increasingly, cross-frontier trading in direct insurance has ceased to be an alternative to establishment. A growing number of governments have prohibited residents from insuring with foreign insurers not authorized to transact insurance business within the country; most countries impose similar restrictions in relation to compulsory insurances, such as motor insurance and workers' compensation insurance. Constraints on establishment, alongside restrictions on cross-frontier business, therefore, considerably inhibit the ability of insurance companies to (i) export their services, (ii) handle claims and (iii) provide facilities for their own nationals for the insurance of their overseas risks.

REINSURANCE BUSINESS

Reinsurers do not have the same operational needs for a physical presence in every country from which they acquire business. To write business successfully, a reinsurer needs:

(a) a detailed knowledge of the insurers with whom it is dealing, the business to be reinsured, the particular insurer's and the local market's claims experience of the class(es) of insurance involved and the local market conditions and usages; and

(b) an ability to service the business including, when necessary, facilities for surveying large risks and investigating claims, sometimes at the request of client insurers.

Obviously, it is easier for a reinsurer to service his clients' business and to keep abreast of local market developments if it has a local office.[3] Similarly, regular contact with, and ready access to, a reinsurer is also advantageous to his clients. A continuous local presence is not essential, however, provided the reinsurer can visit clients and/or avail itself of the services of both local or international reinsurance brokers (who themselves have such regular contact with their clients and with the market) and of legal and other experts.

Every improvement in communications brought about by developments in air travel and information technology further reduces the advantages to an international reinsurer of establishing a network of offices in every country from which business is acquired, although for various reasons there is a strong case for being established in the main international reinsurance centres. No improvement in communications, however, can alter certain essential conditions for the efficient, successful conduct of reinsurance business. These conditions include the need for insurers to have freedom of choice to decide on the types of reinsurance programmes best suited to their requirements and to select the reinsurers to supply them, the exclusion of reinsurance transactions from exchange-control restrictions which unreasonably impede the movement of premiums and claims payments and, thirdly, a freedom for reinsurers to maintain control over the investment of their funds.

VOLUME OF INTERNATIONAL TRADE IN
INSURANCE

There are formidable obstacles to the estimation of the foreign supply of direct insurance and reinsurance. Few insurance supervisory authorities require a breakdown of premium income data in sufficient detail to permit an identification of the proportion of direct insurance placed with foreign insurance companies and their subsidiaries. Even less information is available about reinsurance. By analyzing government returns, published accounts of major insurance and reinsurance groups, balance-of-payments statistics and market information, it is possible to obtain very approximate estimates which indicate orders of magnitude and the broad pattern of change over time.

Direct Insurance Trade

Direct insurance supplied by foreign insurers includes both establishment and cross-frontier. Although the earliest international insurance transactions were cross-frontier, insurance through local establishment also has a long history. Insurance companies have for over a century followed their corporate clients abroad to be in a position to supply their insurance needs in the various parts of the world. Even though the initial motivation to set up abroad was often to service these corporate clients, there has been a natural tendency for these overseas branches and subsidiaries to diversify over time to supply indigenous needs.

The share which foreign insurers hold, either by establishment or through cross-frontier transactions, in the domestic direct non-life insurance markets varies substantially. It ranges from zero in countries where the local insurance market is nationalized to 25 per cent or more in other countries, such as Canada, New Zealand, Italy and Greece. Saudi Arabia offers an interesting extreme case in that, until a government-owned insurance enterprise was set up in 1984, no insurance companies could be incorporated in the local market, either by foreign or indigenous interests. Hence 100 per cent of the direct insurances were supplied by foreign insurance enterprises on a cross-frontier basis. Although any estimate is subject to error, the authors calculate that about 11 per cent of the worldwide non-life insurance premiums are written by foreign insurers, mainly through local establishments.

By contrast to non-life insurance, life insurance has historically been much less international in character. Because of the long-term-savings nature of life insurance and because much of it is purchased by individuals, there has been a far stronger tendency for consumers to buy life insurance from national insurance companies. Traditionally, life insurance companies have also been less inclined to establish overseas branches and subsidiaries, partly because of the buoyancy in their own domestic life insurance markets and partly because there has not been the same degree of competitive pressure to service their multinational clients abroad as in non-life insurance. With the exception of some of the major European life insurance companies seeking to secure a stake in the large North American market, and the more recent interest shown by a few of the major American and Canadian life insurance companies in European markets, foreign establishment has had a strong regional bias. Life insurance companies within the European Community have sought expansion in other Community markets, in part encouraged by the Life Establishment Directive;[4] similarly, American and Canadian life insurance companies have penetrated each other's markets and the same applies within the Australian and New Zealand markets. The authors estimate that only 5 per cent of the global life insurance market is supplied by foreign insurance enterprises, although it should be stated that this proportion has been increasing during the 1980s. Overwhelmingly, this has been achieved through local establishments, including acquisitions of small domestic companies. A negligible amount of direct life insurance has been carried out on a cross frontier basis.

Reinsurance Trade

Table 2.1 shows the global non-life reinsurance supplied by both domestic and foreign insurance companies. There is much less reinsurance support needed for life insurance and so it is ignored in the table. The figures for worldwide reinsurance have been taken from *Sigma*, the publication of the Swiss Reinsurance Group. The authors have estimated the proportion of this worldwide non-life reinsurance that is supplied by foreign insurers both on an establishment and cross-frontier basis. It can be seen that the proportion of reinsurance supplied by foreign insurers has increased substantially between 1962 and 1987.

There are several reasons for this. First, the major German and Swiss specialist reinsurance groups, led by the Munich Reinsurance Company and the Swiss Reinsurance Company, expanded their activities in foreign markets sharply from the early 1960s, in part by the acceptance of cross-frontier reinsurance, but mainly through setting up overseas branches and subsidiaries. Their activities were facilitated by strong domestic currencies and technical expertise built up over many years. Second, the major direct insurance groups which also supply reinsurance extended their reinsurance activities in the face of growing demand for reinsurance from developing

TABLE 2.1

Foreign Supply of Non-Life Reinsurance
($ billions)

	1962 *Net Premiums*	*1974* *Net Premiums*	*1987* *Net Premiums*
Worldwide non-life reinsurance	4.2	17.1	75.7
Reinsurance supplied by foreign companies (establishment and cross-frontier)	1.1	5.1	24.5
Reinsurance supplied by foreign companies as % of worldwide reinsurance	26.2%	29.8%	32.4%

SOURCES: *Sigma*, Swiss Reinsurance Group, Zurich, and authors' estimates.

countries and from the captive insurance companies which had been formed by major industrial and commercial corporations to underwrite some of their own risks. Third, there was a growth of reciprocal reinsurance — that is, reinsurance swaps between insurers. This took place both between insurance groups in order to maintain their size and between insurers and state-owned insurance enterprises in developing countries which sought to reduce the foreign-currency cost of acquiring foreign reinsurance. Fourth, the London market including Lloyd's of London, which historically has been a major international supplier of cross-frontier direct insurance, found more and more of its business coming to it in the form of reinsurance. In the early 1960s, Lloyd's of London had a small proportion of reinsurance, but by the early 1980s the majority of its overseas business came in this form.

Estimating Cross-frontier Flows

As well as considering the total volume of international trade in insurance, whether direct or through reinsurance, it would also be of interest to know the importance of cross-frontier business in the total volume of international insurance. The authors have therefore estimated the cross-frontier flows and these estimates are given in Table 2.2. Because of the quality of available information, however, these estimates must be viewed as very approximate. Cross-frontier flows embrace reinsurance and direct insurance. Direct insurance flows include marine and aviation insurances, insurances on large-scale construction risks abroad and some insurances from the United States, technically referred to as 'surplus-line' business.

Even among marine and aviation insurances, which traditionally have been supplied in relatively free international markets, there has been a tendency for these insurances to be supplied more and more in the form of reinsurance rather than direct insurance. Between 1962 and 1974, although cross-frontier premiums increased from about \$1.2 billion to \$3.5 billion, they fell as a proportion of world non-life insurance premiums, from 3.7 per cent to 3.1 per cent. (It is appropriate to relate these cross-frontier flows to non-life insurance in that very little life insurance is conducted on a cross-frontier basis.) One reason for this relative decline is attributable to a greater ability of national insurance markets to supply reinsurance needs from within. But the main reason for the decline has been the tendency for the major specialist reinsurance groups to set up branches, subsidiaries and associate companies in national markets to service their growing reinsurance business in these markets. Hence, cross-frontier reinsurance was, during 1962-74, being replaced by reinsurance through establishment.

The pattern from 1974-87 shows an increase in the proportion of cross-frontier flows to global non-life insurance. The pattern of large professional reinsurance groups supplying reinsurances through local establishments continued. But this was more than offset by the growth of cross-frontier business attributable to the rapid expansion of off-shore insurance companies and risk sharing pools which, since most of them are registered in tax havens such as Bermuda, give rise to

TABLE 2.2

Global Cross-frontier Insurance/Reinsurance Flows
($ billions)

	1962 *Gross premiums*	*1974* *Gross premiums*	*1987* *Gross premiums*
Global cross-frontier non-life direct insurance and reinsurance	1.2	3.5	18.0
Global demand for non-life insurance	32.4	114.1	524.9
Cross frontier flows as a % of global non-life insurance demand	3.7%	3.1%	3.4%

SOURCE: Authors' estimates.

cross-frontier flows. Premium flows relating to off-shore insurance is estimated at approximately $11 billion in 1987. Technically speaking, a large part of these flows are cross-frontier direct insurance because they represent insurance premiums paid by multinationals and their worldwide subsidiaries to their own off-shore captive insurance companies and to risk sharing pools. Some of the premiums received in these off-shore markets are retained, but a larger proportion is transferred back, either into the national markets in which the parent companies are located or into the wider international market in the form of reinsurance. The growth of reciprocal reinsurance agreements, noted earlier, also contributed in part to the buoyancy of the cross-frontier flows during the late 1970s and the 1980s.

It is clear that international trade in insurance, whether conducted on an establishment or cross-frontier basis, is small in relation to both total world premium expenditure and international transactions in many other industries.[5] The share of foreign insurers varies considerably from country to country, but it has been growing in recent years mainly through cross border take-overs. Nevertheless, there is no indication that the removal of all restrictions would lead to a dramatic overall increase. There are three reasons for this:

(a) insurance operations do not lend themselves to the large economies of scale that would enable a few giant companies to dominate world trade, as in some other industries; and

(b) consumers generally prefer to deal with local companies although sometimes a foreign insurer's reputation may be such as to overcome the obstacle.

(c) cross border take-overs are becoming more difficult because of a reduced availability of insurance companies for purchase at acceptable prices.

However, the benefits to be derived from freer international insurance and reinsurance trade are substantial, as we shall discuss later in the study.

NOTES AND REFERENCES

1. Even the American insurance industry resorts to international reinsurance to provide the capacity required for large risks. United States reinsurance premiums paid abroad accounted for 4 per cent

of total non-life premiums in 1989.

2. For a fuller discussion, see Robert L. Carter, 'Multinational Insurance Companies', *Vie et Sciences Economiques*, Paris, January 1976.

3. A.M. Sabbagh, 'Reinsurance Review', *The Review*, London, 9 January 1984.

4. The directive facilitated the implementation of 'freedom of establishment' whereby an insurer established and authorized to transact life insurance in one member state was given the right to establish branch offices in other member countries.

5. For example, it was estimated a long while ago that the output of foreign-controlled subsidiaries in primary and manufacturing industries substantially exceeds the value of world merchandise trade. David Robertson, 'Operations of Multinational Enterprises in Perspective', in Hugh Corbet and Robert Jackson (eds), *In Search of a New World Economic Order* (London: Croom Helm, for the Trade Policy Research Centre, 1974).

Chapter 3

Objectives of Barriers to Trade in Insurance

RESTRICTIONS on international trade in insurance fall under two main headings:

(a) barriers to the local establishment of foreign or foreign-owned insurance companies; and

(b) restrictions or other measures detrimental to the placing abroad of insurances or reinsurances with foreign insurers established abroad.

In each case, the restrictions take a variety of forms and, as indicated in Chapter 1, not all are attributable to government action alone. Rather than attempting to deal in detail with the restrictions applied by individual countries, analyses of the main types of restriction, including details for a representative number of countries, are given in Appendix I.

Before examining the different types of restriction, it is appropriate to consider the stated objectives of governments and other bodies that have led to the imposition of restrictions on international trade in insurance. Apart from political reasons, the objectives can be grouped broadly under six headings:

(a) to protect domestic policyholders from loss in the event of insurance companies becoming insolvent or their failure to provide an acceptable standard of service at a reasonable price;

(b) to avoid wasteful and destructive competition between insurers principally for the purpose of protecting policyholders' interests;

(c) to build up a local insurance market by protecting domestic insurers from foreign competition;

(d) to avoid unnecessary loss of foreign exchange either through the purchase of insurance/reinsurance from abroad or through the remittance of funds abroad by foreign or foreign-owned insurance companies;

(e) to ensure that funds generated by insurance operations are directed into the local capital market; and

(f) to reduce, for reasons of national security, the country's dependence on the supply of foreign insurance and/or reinsurance.

Restrictions on foreign insurance, therefore, can either be part of a government's overall development strategy[1] or part of a general policy of consumer protection.

PROTECTION OF POLICYHOLDERS

Insurance provides, at the time of sale, only a promise of future performance. Thus, the insurer undertakes if and when a claim is made, to deal with it fairly and to have sufficient funds to settle the claim in full. In the case of life insurance that promise may not need to be fulfilled for twenty or more years ahead. Also, liability and some other classes of non-life insurance are subject to long delays in settlement and sometimes in the notification of claims as well (for example, in the case of industrial diseases). Should the insurer default for any reason, the financial consequences may be very serious for the policyholder and possibly for other persons as well, such as dependants or injured third parties.

Throughout the world, governments have legislated to protect policyholders from incompetent and unscrupulous insurers. Such legislation usually includes the following elements:

(a) A system under which companies have to be licensed to transact insurance business. Applicants usually have to satisfy the supervisory authority as to their solvency, their competence and their financial and business integrity. Some countries prohibit companies from transacting both life and non-life insurance in order to prevent the savings of life policyholders from being used to pay for losses on other classes of insurance.

(b) Minimum capital requirements including the frequent valuation of assets and liabilities on pre-determined bases.

(c) The regular preparation and publication of accounts in a prescribed form.

(d) Regulations relating to the conduct of the business such as the company's reinsurance arrangements, policy coverage and conditions, premium rating and so on.

(e) Control of the investment of insurance funds, including regulations relating to eligible types of assets, portfolio composition and the deposit of securities.

(f) Regulations governing the winding-up of companies that fail to meet any of the prescribed standards of solvency or behaviour, including adequate compensation schemes for policyholders.

Such regulations governing the establishment of insurance companies may directly or indirectly discriminate against foreign or foreign-owned companies.

The desire to protect policyholders may also induce a government to constrain residents from placing their insurances abroad on the grounds that it can exercise no control over the behaviour or solvency of companies not established in the country. Similarly, legislation making certain classes of liability insurance compulsory usually stipulates that, in order to protect the interests of third parties, the insurance shall be effected only with an authorized insurer.

The case for protecting policyholders from the consequences of a 'bad buy' is more persuasive in relation to individuals and small traders than for companies and other large buyers of insurance. Provided insurers are required to publish adequate information about their financial affairs, large buyers of insurance should either possess, or should be able to obtain, sufficient information about the solvency and reputation of any insurance company, whether domestic or foreign, to make official constraints on freedom of choice unnecessary and undesirable. The problem is to frame legislation which protects individuals from the consequences of their ignorance without hampering the freedom of those large buyers who are fully aware of the pitfalls.

AVOIDANCE OF WASTEFUL AND DESTRUCTIVE COMPETITION

Competition has the same beneficial effects in insurance markets as in other industries in that it acts as a spur to efficiency and to innovation in product design and in methods of production and distribution. On the other hand, competition is not without costs. Not only are additional resources wasted in two or more companies competing for the same business but, most important, there is the danger of intensive competition undermining company solvency and thus the security provided for policyholders. Underwriters when fixing premiums, particularly for non-life insurance, cannot avoid making subjective judgements regarding future conditions and, almost inevitably, companies eager to expand their market share may take an over-optimistic view of trends in claims, administrative expenses and/or investment yields.

Under-estimation of claims poses the greatest problem, particularly in classes of insurance where the probability of a loss is very small but the severity of loss is very large (for example, earthquake or war risks), or where there are sudden permanent increases in the level of claim costs such as in product liability and professional indemnity insurances. The history of insurance shows that when no large claims occur for a while there is an endemic market tendency for insurance premiums in these classes of insurance to fall below their economic cost; this is often caused by the entry of new insurance companies into the market endeavouring to gain a foothold through 'competitive' pricing. When large insured losses occur, whether insurers are forced into liquidation or not, insurance premiums rise sharply for a while, sometimes above their new economic level as insurers try to recoup some of the unforeseen losses already incurred. This sudden increase in premiums is destabilizing to the market in the short term as demand for insurance can be deterred until consumers adjust to the new market conditions. A recent example of this is the rapid increase in premiums during 1985 (in some cases exceeding 100 per cent) for professional indemnity insurance in the United Kingdom following judgments of negligence against accountants and the suppliers of professional services; these judgments led to large compensation payments which eventually were paid by insurance companies.

Price competition, whether it is brought about by design or by ignorance of risk costs, can be controlled in various ways. A government may directly control premium rates (perhaps requiring all established insurers to adhere to agreed minimum tariff rates) or exclude external competition by prohibiting the placing of insurances abroad. Alternatively, if it believes that the fault lies in too many insurers competing for the limited amount of business available, it may seek to curtail their number. Economic theory does not conclusively support the argument that a reduction in the number of competitors will lessen competition and lead to market stability, but an examination of insurance market structures and behaviour gives some credence to the proposition.[2] Perhaps competition does need to be restrained occasionally, but it must be recognized that restraints on competition are likely to lead to consumer losses if competition is replaced by monopoly.[3]

DEVELOPMENT OF LOCAL INSURANCE MARKETS

Various reasons are advanced, particularly by developing countries, for the development of a strong local insurance industry as a way of reducing a country's dependence upon foreign insurers. Not only are there potential balance-of-payments benefits to be derived from business being handled by local insurers, but a local insurance industry would also assist in the diversification of the economy. In addition, it would be possible to maintain local control over an industry that, in many aspects of its operations, is vital to economic growth and welfare. As they require little investment in fixed capital, insurance services are eminently suitable for local production.

The need for protection is based usually on two arguments. First, in the initial stages of development there is the need to protect small, newly-established companies from giant multinational insurance companies which enjoy benefits of scale from their extensive global operations (the infant-industry argument). Second, at the next stage, it is argued that a high density of insurance companies operating in a market leads to wasteful competition. There is also a risk that competition would not only be wasteful but also destructive in the sense that it could undermine the solvency of some (possibly local) companies. Foreign insurers, able to cross-subsidize their operations in different countries, can better withstand and may initiate such competition.

The long-term dangers inherent in the infant-industry argument are too well-known to repeat here.[4] The support provided by economic theory for the second line of argument is too inconclusive to justify either its universal applicability or its use as a justification for discrimination against foreign insurers. It is possible that foreign insurance companies with their wider experience may seek to exercise a stabilizing influence in the market. Nor, for that matter, does the first argument stand up to examination for insurance companies need to be in a position to spread risks as widely as possible. This will be dealt with later.

PROTECTION FOR THE BALANCE OF PAYMENTS

The insurance or reinsurance of local risks with foreign insurers can affect a country's balance of payments in various ways which can sometimes be complex.[5] Short-term current and capital flows may be either positive or negative because of variations in payments of insurance claims, but over the longer term a country that imports insurance services can expect the first order effects to be as follows:

(a) Insurances or reinsurances placed with insurers located abroad will over time lead to an outflow of premium payments which will be only partly offset by claim inflows. Even if funds required to cover expected claims and local expenses are maintained in the country, contributions to central reserves and profits will be remitted abroad.

(b) When foreign insurers or reinsurers are established within the country, profits earned will through time be remitted to the parent head office. The local company may also heavily reinsure with its parent and this will create the same effect as in (a). In addition 'free' reserves may be sent to the head office for centralized investment.

The actual strain on a country's balance of payments, though, may be less than it appears at first sight. Much depends upon the class of insurance concerned and the contribution that domestic resources, which otherwise would have been utilized in the provision of insurance, can make to exports or other forms of import-saving. The remaining foreign-exchange cost may be further reduced by a countervailing inflow of funds from reciprocal reinsurance arrangements with foreign companies. The overwhelming majority of countries, however, remain net importers of insurance.[6] Whether the net long-term foreign exchange cost is a reasonable price to pay must be judged in relation to the benefit obtained from reducing the economic disturbances which a country would otherwise suffer because of the inability of local insurance companies to meet possible contingencies through a lack of liquid reserves.

The investment abroad of reserve funds, whether by insurers established within a country or by remitting direct insurance or reinsurance premiums abroad, is like any other outflow of funds for foreign portfolio investment. Initially, there will be an outflow of funds on the balance-of-payments capital account which may exert further downward pressure on the exchange rate of a weak currency. Subsequently, however, a countervailing investment earnings inflow on the current account will occur. For example, if premiums are remitted abroad for life insurance, the ultimate claims receipts would normally be greater than the aggregate premium payments — the difference being the investment earnings on the accumulating funds held abroad over the years.

CHANNELLING FUNDS TO LOCAL CAPITAL MARKETS

The manner in which insurance companies conduct their operations inevitably leads to the accumulation of funds over and above the capital subscribed by shareholders. In all classes of insurance business a time lag occurs between the payment of premiums and the settlement of claims so that the insurer holds funds to cover his liabilities to policyholders. In general, life insurance is conducted on a level premium basis; that is, policyholders pay premiums during the early years of their contract in excess of the sum required to cover the mortality risk so that a fund is built up to meet the excess of claims over premium income in later years.

Non-life policies are usually written on an annual basis, the policyholder paying a premium at inception to cover the risk of losses which may occur at any time during the year. In some classes of insurance there is often a substantial delay between the occasion of the loss and the final settlement of the claim.[7] While an insurer's business is expanding, it is usually able to meet most claims and administrative costs out of current premium income, so that the funds required to cover his liabilities to policyholders in effect roll forward from year to year and are available for investment.

The long-term nature of life insurance means that policyholders' funds are far larger in relation to their annual premium income than in the case of general insurance.[8] Indeed, they often comprise a major part of personal savings within a country.

If insurances are placed abroad with foreign insurers with no restrictions on the remittance of premiums, the accumulating funds will be lost to the local capital market. Even if foreign insurers are established locally, they are more likely than local companies to remit at least part of their funds abroad, possibly for investment by their head offices. Thus restrictions on the import of insurance services and on the establishment of foreign insurers may be seen as a means of retaining a substantial source of funds for investment through the local capital market. Such funds could be channelled into government securities or used to finance new agricultural, industrial and commercial projects in the private sector of the economy.

Any action taken by a government to protect its economy from an outflow of capital is understandable, especially in a country where economic development may be hindered by a scarcity of funds. Nevertheless, adequate safeguards can be devised without having to resort to the exclusion of trade with foreign insurers. It will be explained later, however, that even less drastic measures, designed merely to retain funds at home, may be contrary to the best interests of policyholders and, in certain circumstances, to the economy at large.

NATIONAL SECURITY

On occasions it is argued that governments may wish to build up their domestic insurance industries for reasons of national security even if the costs may exceed, other than in the event of war, the economic benefits. For example, Harold Skipper, a professor of insurance in the United States, cites the Arab region's commercial vulnerability to the decisions of the London marine insurance market which, it was said, prompted the formation of two large Arab insurance groups. Marine and aviation cover on Argentine ships, aircraft and cargo was also suspended or curtailed by London insurers and reinsurers during the Falkland Islands conflict.[9]

How large are the costs which a government is willing to incur in the interests of national security is a political, not an economic decision. Nevertheless, in making such decisions, account should be taken of alternative sources of supply; if the country is highly dependent on one source, consideration should be given to the possibility of spreading its demand amongst a wider range of suppliers. Apart from a nation that faces the risk of worldwide trade sanctions, the threats to national security from a high dependence upon insurance/reinsurance imports are small given the numbers of insurers and reinsurers from many countries that are active in the international insurance and reinsurance markets and the ability of insurers to supply their services instantly. Evidence of this is given by the fact that the Argentine Government was able to arrange for the continuance of cover during the Falklands War through the National Reinsurance Institute (INDER) which had access to alternative sources of reinsurance.

NOTES AND REFERENCES

1. It has been argued that developing countries have been motivated principally by objectives (d) and (e), although some claim that premium rates charged by international insurers have been excessively high. See W.R. Malinowski, 'European Insurance and the Third World', *Journal of World Trade Law*, Geneva, August-September 1971; and José Ripoll, 'UNCTAD and Insurance', *Journal of World Trade Law*, January-February 1974. In the mid-1970s, more emphasis was placed on the need for developing countries to diversify their economies and on the suitability of insurance for national control. See Ripoll, 'Some Thoughts on Development and Insurance', *Best's Review*, Oldwick, New Jersey, February 1976.

2. For example, the Superintendent of Insurance for Canada stated in 1964 that over the previous ten-year period premiums had been inadequate and threatened the potential of some insurance companies to pay claims; he attributed the inadequacy of premiums primarily to the large number of companies in the market. *Report of the Superintendent of Insurance for Canada for the Year Ending 31 December 1964* (Ottawa: Queens Printer, 1965).

3. It has been observed that 'the German insurance regulations impose quite high costs in terms of loss of efficiency with no significant increase in the benefit given to consumers either in the level of protection they afford them or in alleviating the problem

of imperfect information'. With regard to price regulation, it has been shown that the prices of German term life insurances are much higher than in the unregulated United Kingdom market. Finsinger, Hammond and Tapp, *op. cit.*, pp. 169-170.

4. Harry G. Johnson, 'Optimal Trade Intervention in the Presence of Domestic Distortions', in Robert E. Caves *et al.*, *Trade, Growth and Balance of Payments* (Amsterdam: North Holland, 1965); and Caves and R.W. Jones, *World Trade and Payments* (Boston, Massachusetts: Little, Brown, 1973) p. 260.

5. An extensive discussion and analysis of balance-of-payments effects can be found in Gerard M. Dickinson, *International Insurance Transactions and the Balance of Payments*, Geneva Papers on Risk and Insurance No. 6 (Geneva: Association Internationale pour l'Etude de l'Economie de l'Assurance, 1977).

6. Only the United Kingdom and Switzerland have consistently been net exporters of insurance and reinsurance in recent years. See Dickinson, *op. cit.* During the 1980s reinsurance premiums received from abroad by American companies averaged less than one-third of the reinsurance premiums they paid to foreign reinsurers.

7. G. Clayton and W.T. Osborne, *Insurance Company Investment* (London: Allen & Unwin, 1965) ch. 3.

8. For example, at the end of 1984 the ratio of the long-term (life) invested funds to the premium income of United Kingdom insurance companies was 8.3:1 compared with a ratio of 1.9:1 for general insurance business. *Insurance Facts and Figures* (London: British Insurance Association, 1985). The ratio for American life companies, whose business has a smaller savings element than the United Kingdom companies, was 5.4:1. *Life Insurance Fact Book* (Washington: American Council of Life Insurance, 1985).

9. Harold D. Skipper; 'Protectionism in the Provision of International Insurance Services', *Journal of Risk and Insurance*, Orlando, Vol. LIV, No. 1, 1987.

Chapter 4

Types of Restrictions Imposed on Insurance Trade

REFERENCE HAS already been made to the proliferation of restrictions on trade in insurance and reinsurance since the 1950s. It would be a massive task, therefore, to attempt to compile a detailed list of the numerous restrictions which many countries have seen fit to impose, ranging from the total exclusion of foreign insurers from the local direct insurance business to measures which simply add to the costs for buyers and/or sellers. For example, the 1983 report from the Organisation for Economic Cooperation and Development (OECD) on international trade in insurance[1] contains 26 pages of tables summarizing the obstacles imposed by its member countries. This summary is not exhaustive, however, as the report revealed the need for a number of measures and practices to be studied in more detail. Moreover, government measures are always subject to change so that the most comprehensive list would soon be outdated.[2]

In this chapter, therefore, the main types of restrictions are described in broad terms; the precise details will vary from case to case. What is more, a country may employ a combination of different measures to achieve its objectives and will often discriminate between various classes of insurance business. The common feature is that the majority of countries recognize the case for more liberal treatment of reinsurance transactions and generally, fewer restrictions are placed on reinsurance than on direct insurance.

DIRECT BARRIERS TO CROSS-FRONTIER INSURANCE

There are four main types of direct barrier which countries impose in order to prevent insurance business being placed with foreign insurers. They are (i) restrictions on the freedom of residents to place insurance abroad, (ii) government procurement practices, (iii) exchange-control regulations and (iv) restrictions on reinsurance. Each of these will be discussed in turn.

Restrictions on Insuring Abroad

In many countries there is legislation which prohibits residents (individuals or corporations) from placing their insurances with foreign insurers not licensed to transact insurance business within the country; penalties are imposed on anyone who does so.

Certain classes of insurance tend to be compulsory, notably third-party liability insurance for the owners and/or users of motor vehicles; usually the insurance must be effected with an insurer who is authorized to transact that class of business within the country.[3] In some cases, compulsory insurances must be placed with a state-owned insurance organization.[4] As the object of compulsory insurance provisions is to try to guarantee that, in the event of loss, adequate funds will be available to compensate the victim, especially innocent third parties, it is understandable that governments should require the insurance to be provided by an insurance company over which it can exercise control.

In many cases,[5] however, legislation prohibiting insuring abroad extends beyond compulsory insurances, sometimes embracing all classes of insurance. Enforcement of this legislation, however, can present great difficulties. For example, multinational groups operating within a country may apparently carry their own risks locally, but in reality the parent company may protect its interest by arranging insurance on its home market. Alternatively, it may persuade a local insurer to 'front' the insurance — that is, to issue the policy in compliance with local law, but then to reinsure 90 per cent or more of the risk abroad, possibly with a 'captive' insurance company owned by the multinational for the purpose of insuring its own risks.[6] Likewise, a government can exercise little or no control over the insurance arrangements of the overseas subsidiary and associated companies of its own national companies, especially if they are subject to local insurance regulations. Finally, considerable difficulties can arise with transport insurances. Other measures, such as tax regulations, may be introduced to make evasion less attractive, but absolute compliance can never be guaranteed.

In some countries, if the local market is unwilling, or does not have the capacity to cover certain risks, approval may be sought from the insurance supervisory authority to place the insurance abroad.[7] Permission, however, may be granted only in exceptional circumstances and even then heavy taxes may be imposed. Again, difficulties may arise where local insurers are prepared to offer cover, but the terms are often so unreasonable as to make the insurance either uneconomic or otherwise unacceptable.

Controls on the placing of transport insurances create particular problems. Besides indirect controls through taxation, terms of import licences and exchange-control regulations, the two forms of direct control are: (i) a requirement that imports be insured in the receiving country,[8] and (ii) a requirement that exports be insured in the country of origin.[9]

Although the United Nations Conference on Trade and Development (UNCTAD) encourages developing countries to retain, for their own insurance markets, as much as possible of the transport insurance which their international trading activities generate, a study by the UNCTAD Secretariat recognized the wider issues involved.[10] Such issues include the general terms on which international trade is conducted, the conflicting aims of importers and exporters and their countries with the consequent risk of double insurance being effected and, thirdly the technical and organizational problems which insurers in developing countries would have to overcome in order to offer an efficient insurance service.

Government Procurement Practices

Discrimination is practised in some countries in favour of domestic insurance companies and against foreign ones by governments bringing pressure to bear on government departments, local authorities, public enterprises and private concerns which depend on government patronage, to deal with locally-owned (sometimes only the state-owned) insurance companies.[11] The larger the public sector the greater the impact such measures have on foreign insurers. Moreover such government procurement practices affect locally-established foreign or foreign-owned insurers. These practices, together with other operational constraints, were ranked by the OECD as the second most serious obstacle to trade.[12]

Exchange-control Regulations

Another direct method employed by governments to prevent the import of insurance services is through the control of foreign exchange. Even if the placing of insurance abroad is not prohibited, most residents are effectively prevented from doing so if they cannot obtain the necessary foreign exchange for the remission of premiums to overseas insurers.[13] There is, of course, always the possibility that persons or companies in receipt of incomes abroad may be able to obtain the necessary funds to pay the premiums. They may, however, be deterred from doing so by exchange-control regulations or tax provisions governing the treatment of insurance claims proceeds.

Insurance cross-frontier business may also be hampered by exchange-control regulations imposed by the home governments of foreign insurers. Regulations prohibiting insurers from retaining, in original currencies, premiums received on overseas risks may be introduced despite the fact that insurers are only trying to build up foreign-currency reserves to meet expected claims. In a period of floating exchange rates, insurers and reinsurers may be reluctant to assume the ensuing exchange-rate risks, particularly if their home currency is expected to depreciate relative to the currencies in which payments will have to be made.

Reinsurance

Domestic insurance companies are generally allowed more freedom to place their reinsurances abroad. Reinsurance transactions are subject to less stringent exchange-control regulations than those applied to direct insurance transactions. Nevertheless, some countries limit the freedom of domestic insurance companies in various ways.[14]

First, all insurers operating within the country may be required to reinsure with a local, usually state-owned, reinsurance corporation.[15] The scope of such regulations varies in degree depending on:

(a) whether locally-established insurance companies offering direct insurance, including foreign-owned companies, are permitted to formulate their own reinsurance policies or are obliged to cede[16] to the local reinsurance corporation a specified share of all business written; and

(b) whether the companies retain some freedom to reinsure with other reinsurance companies, including foreign companies, or must place all their reinsurances with the local state-owned corporation which alone is permitted to retrocede[17] risks abroad.

In some cases where a degree of freedom is left to insurance companies supplying direct insurance, foreign-owned companies are subject to more stringent regulations than locally-owned companies.[18]

Second, insurance companies offering direct insurance may be required to place all or part of certain classes of insurance they underwrite with a local or regional pool.[19] The pool may be organized as a separate reinsurance company in which the participating member companies are shareholders or as an administrative body responsible for redistributing the total business written amongst the members in agreed proportions. Whatever the method, the result is that the business available to international reinsurers will be reduced substantially.

INDIRECT BARRIERS TO CROSS-FRONTIER INSURANCE

In addition to regulations that directly prohibit the placing abroad of domestic insurances (or reinsurances) with insurers (or reinsurers) not licensed to transact business within the country or regulations that directly reduce the flow of business, there are many other types of measures which indirectly hinder cross-frontier trade. These measures adversely affect the ability of foreign insurers (and reinsurers) to compete against domestic companies. Some measures are designed to place foreign insurers on an equal competitive footing with domestic companies. Regulations which allow insurances to be placed with foreign insurers only if the insurance contracts are subject to local law or the requirement that foreign insurers should subscribe to local premium rating agreements (even though that might mean that policyholders are denied the possibility of obtaining their insurances at lower premiums), are measures of this kind. Other measures directly discriminate against foreign insurers in favour of domestic companies by imposing additional financial burdens and costs on the former or on residents who choose to insure or reinsure with them. Such measures take the following forms.

Discriminatory Taxation

Fiscal policies can have a distorting effect on cross-frontier insurance trade. Such policies are aimed at (i) discouraging the import of insurance or (ii) compensating for the loss of tax revenue since the foreign-based insurer or reinsurer is not subject to local corporate taxation. Compensating tax arrangements, such as the withholding from premiums remitted to foreign insurers or reinsurers a tax based on the premium itself or on an imputed amount of profit, also discourage the supply of foreign direct insurance and reinsurance. As these arrangements are often linked directly or indirectly to premium levels rather than to profits, the degree of discouragement to supply tends to be greatest when competition is keen and profit margins are depressed. Moreover, in a number of instances, the omission of such tax levies from double taxation agreements[20] is a further disincentive to the foreign insurer, for he can obtain no tax relief in his own country.

Tax distortions on cross-frontier business in direct insurance assume a variety of forms. In some countries a tax is levied on insurance premiums; this tax is paid by the individual or company taking out the insurance. This particular tax may be used as a discriminatory measure in that it may be levied at a higher rate on insurances placed outside the local market. The differential is sometimes small,[21] but it can often be so sizeable as to have a substantial impact on relative prices or expected profit margins.[22] Sometimes, a fiscal distortion takes a less explicit form either by not allowing domestic policy-holders to charge premiums paid to foreign insurers as tax deductible expenses, although such concessions exist in respect of premiums paid to domestic insurers,[23] or by treating claims receipts under such policies as income and thus subject to tax.

In the case of reinsurance transactions, tax distortions take on more complex guises. The distortions may have the effect of increasing the corporate tax paid by a domestic ceding insurer over what it would be if the reinsurance had been placed locally. This can be done by limiting the amount of the reinsurance premium paid to overseas reinsurers that can be offset against overall premiums in assessing local corporate tax liability.[24] The tax distortion can also arise in the form of a higher level of tax effectively being imposed on the foreign supplier of reinsurance (as in the case of direct insurances).[25]

Overseas Reinsurances

Insurance supervisory regulations may impose other costs on domestic insurance companies who reinsure with non-admitted foreign reinsurers. In some countries the regulations for calculating the provisions for the unearned portion of the premiums of policies that extend beyond the end of an insurance company's financial year and the provisions for reported claims still awaiting settlement at that date, discriminate against non-admitted foreign reinsurers. Whereas an insurer may be permitted to take credit for the liabilities it has transferred to locally-established reinsurers, no such deduction from the required provisions may be allowed for reinsurances placed abroad with foreign reinsurers. Consequently, if an insurance company chooses to reinsure abroad, unless it can persuade foreign reinsurers to deposit with it their share of the unearned premium and outstanding claims reserves, it will need to be more highly capitalized in order to meet the supervisory authority's minimum solvency requirement than if all of its reinsurances were placed locally.[26] Normally, insurance companies maintain capital reserves well in excess of the statutory minimum margins, but legislation of this kind can still have a significant effect when solvency margins are temporarily under pressure because of a depressed level in financial asset values and the cost of raising additional external capital is high.

Localization of Reserves

Legislation aimed at withholding payment of premiums due to foreign insurers and reinsurers can act as a barrier to the supply of cross-frontier insurances and reinsurances whether such legislation is motivated by a concern for the welfare of the policyholder or by balance-of-payments considerations. Such legislation can be considered discriminatory because of both the additional capital costs which will be incurred if reserves have to be held locally and the extra currency risks that overseas suppliers of insurance and reinsurance will have to bear.

Often, in the case of reinsurance, the ceding insurer must either retain premium balances locally, because of insurance supervisory or exchange-control regulations, or negotiate with the reinsurer to do so for solvency-margin reasons discussed earlier. Ceding companies also frequently ask for reserves held to cover claims under proportional reinsurance treaties to be deposited locally.

Given a system of floating exchange rates, few insurers or reinsurers would object strongly to the localization of funds, provided deposits are based on a realistic valuation of expected claims costs and can be invested to provide the same level of return as is available to local companies. Indeed, many companies tend to follow a policy of currency matching of assets and liabilities in order to minimize their foreign-exchange risks. If, however, required deposits far exceed the estimated liability and/or below-market rates of interest are paid on them, then it is argued that such restrictions are more injurious to international reinsurance transactions than to direct insurance business.

Generally, the portfolio of business which a reinsurer writes in a given country will be smaller and have a less stable claims experience than that for a direct insurer. This is particularly true of reinsurance portfolios comprising mainly non-proportional reinsurances exposed to catastrophe losses. The same degree of currency matching cannot be achieved and reinsurers need to be able to transfer funds between countries to meet losses when and where they occur. In such conditions one way of minimizing exchange-rate risks is to maintain a substantial part of the funds in 'strong' currencies;[27] the localization of reserves may prevent a reinsurer from taking such precautions.

Deposit regulations which extend beyond the provision for unearned premiums and outstanding claims are harmful to both insurers and reinsurers. 'Locked-in' funds cannot contribute to the level and cost of maintaining the mobile central capital fund which a multinational insurance company needs to meet the potential catastrophe losses which might arise anywhere in the world. Again, reinsurers probably suffer most because of the more unstable character of the business they tend to write. This capital problem is compounded also by the fact that management and other expenses incurred by the foreign insurer or reinsurer have to be financed from internal sources or from additional capital raising outside the country concerned.

Finally, in some countries foreign insurers are required to hold their locked-in funds in financial assets which have a low yield; this puts the foreign company at a disadvantage *vis-à-vis* domestic insurers.[28] The major part, if not all, of the profits earned on life and non-life business arises from investment earnings and insurers are concerned to obtain the highest rate of return possible, consistent with an acceptable level of risk.

Obstacles such as those outlined have tended to be associated with countries suffering from 'weak' currencies on foreign-exchange markets. Similar problems have arisen, however, in countries with strong currencies, such as Switzerland, where exchange-control regulations have been used to discourage inward portfolio investment by non-residents through the use of low or even negative interest rates. Foreign reinsurers are thus unable to earn an investment return on funds held by a domestic ceding insurer whereas domestic reinsurers can earn the market rate of return.

Restrictions on Non-admitted Insurances

Like any other form of commercial transaction, disputes inevitably arise between the parties to an insurance contract. If insurances placed abroad with foreign insurers are treated as illegal and, thereby, the contract is unenforceable in the courts of the policyholder's own country, there will be an added incentive for residents to look to locally-established insurers.

Similarly, any measures which impair the services which foreign insurers or brokers can provide will act as an obstacle to trade. For example, in many countries local insurance agents and brokers are prohibited from placing insurances abroad with insurers not licensed to transact such business in the country concerned, even though in some cases (for example, Belgium, Luxembourg and the Federal Republic of

Germany) residents may approach the foreign insurers direct.[29] The infringement of such regulations may lead not only to the punishing of the offending broker, the insurer may also be penalized. For example, if a foreign insurer licensed to write certain classes of insurance in the Federal Republic accepts in another country any other class of insurance offered by a German broker, the licence of the foreign insurer may be terminated.[30] Other measures which serve to restrict cross-frontier trade are regulations which prohibit foreign insurers from using the services of local loss adjusters to handle claims. Also, restrictions on advertising serve to isolate a foreign insurer from most of the insuring public.

DIRECT BARRIERS TO ESTABLISHMENT
BUSINESS
As already argued, a foreign insurance company will need to have a local presence if it is to compete effectively against local companies and transact in any country a substantial volume of business, particularly personal and small business insurances. Therefore, although the need for a local establishment is not so important for a reinsurer as for an insurer dealing in direct insurance, the measures which restrict the freedom of foreign insurers to appoint general (underwriting) agents or to set up branch offices or subsidiaries in any country may be viewed as the most serious obstacles to international insurance trade. That was the conclusion reached by the OECD after reviewing both the nature of insurance operations and the number and severity of restrictions.[31]

The restrictions will be considered under the two headings of direct and indirect barriers. It may be noted that sometimes less stringent obstacles apply to the establishment of subsidiaries than to the establishment of branches. The direct barriers are dealt with first.

Nationalization
State appropriation of insurance business previously in the hands of the private sector may be achieved in two ways:

(a) by incorporating certain classes of insurance into a country's social-security arrangements; and

(b) by total or partial nationalization — either by an outright take-over by a state-owned company of all of the business of private companies or of certain classes of insurance (for example, compulsory motor insurance) or alternatively all private companies could be prohibited from operating in the country and the state corporation would be given a monopoly of the insurance business.

Whatever the method used, private insurers lose all or part of their portfolios of direct insurance business.

Many countries have introduced social-security schemes providing compensation, in varying degrees, for sickness and personal injury caused by industrial and other accidents.[32] As a result, private insurers have lost a substantial volume of business. Domestic and foreign-owned companies, however, are equally affected by such measures and therefore they do not fall within the scope of this study. It is also argued by proponents that not only do such measures provide more rational methods of compensating the victims of accidents but also the nature of the risks are such that there is no economic necessity for a country to seek to spread the costs beyond its own boundaries.

In a number of countries (for example, in some of the provinces of Canada and in some Australian states) state-owned insurance offices have been given a monopoly of compulsory motor and workers' compensation insurance previously handled by private insurers.

In most cases where governments have decided to nationalize insurance business, the policy has been one of complete nationalization of both domestic and foreign companies.[33] But there have been some notable exceptions.

In 1946 the French Government nationalized only some of the French-owned companies leaving the remainder, together with the foreign companies established in France, to compete against the state-owned companies. When Portugal nationalized its insurance industry in 1975, only locally-owned companies were taken over. Egypt, which nationalized its insurance industry in 1956, has now not only re-admitted to its domestic market Egyptian-owned private companies it has also formed the free zone with provision for the establishment of joint-venture companies with foreign participation although not control.

Restrictions on Foreign-owned Companies

The establishment of foreign insurance companies in the local market can be restricted in two ways:

   (a) by prohibiting the entry of new companies to the market and possibly restricting the development of companies already established; and more generally

   (b) by excluding foreign-controlled companies.

In 1911, Uruguay gave her State Insurance Bank a monopoly of all insurance business; foreign-owned companies already operating in the country were permitted to continue, but only for classes of business they were already writing. As mentioned, Portugal nationalized the locally-owned companies, although foreign insurers already established were allowed to continue in business. However, following Portugal's entry to the EEC it has had to reopen its market to Community insurers, and more recently has had to accept other EC insurers as potential owners of these state insurance companies under its privatization programme.

The supervisory laws of most countries now use systems of licensing to control the entry of new insurance companies to their insurance markets and also, in many cases, the extension of the activities of existing companies into different classes of insurance business.[34] Equal treatment of domestic and foreign applicants under such laws goes to the root of freedom of establishment; without the right to apply for a new or extended licence, other detailed licensing and operational rules discussed below are without significance.

Where the same rules apply to both locally-owned and foreign companies, unless the rules are administered in a discriminatory manner, there are few grounds for complaint, although countries that do allow foreign insurers to enter their markets may seek to negotiate reciprocal agreements affording equal treatment for their insurers. It would appear, however, that discriminatory treatment of foreign applicants is often a problem. One of the regular causes for complaint by foreign insurers is the inordinate delay by some countries in the handling of applications for licences.[35]

It has become increasingly common for companies wishing to establish in a country by opening a branch office to be prohibited, or at least discouraged, from doing so. Moreover, it has become quite common for countries to limit entry to the local insurance market to locally-owned companies and also to require foreign insurers already operating in the country to convert their organizations to locally-registered companies.[36] The general principle of the domestication of insurance business is discussed more fully below, but it is noteworthy that in a growing number of cases the legislation provides for the control of all insurance companies to be exercised locally by requiring management posts, and/or a majority of the shares, to be held by nationals.[37]

INDIRECT BARRIERS TO ESTABLISHMENT

BUSINESS

The indirect barriers imposed by many countries are often more effective in deterring insurance companies from setting up a branch or subsidiary in another country. Four particular barriers are considered here: (i) restrictions placed on the freedom of foreign companies to remit profits to the parent company, (ii) the use of discriminatory taxation by the host country, (iii) restrictions on the employment of expatriates and (iv) discriminatory market practices.

Restrictions on Remittances

A common feature of a number of insurance markets, particularly those in developing countries, is the system of exchange-control restrictions on the remittance of funds. These may take the form of a direct restriction on the transfer of funds, or delays in obtaining permission from the local authorities to transfer funds; these delays can be long and irregular.[38]

The extent to which exchange controls on remittances are discriminatory is not clear-cut since these controls also apply to domestic companies. It would seem appropriate, however, to define exchange controls as discriminatory when they limit, delay or permit only at a penal exchange rate remittances abroad of profits and/or payments for management services provided by the head office of the parent organization for the benefit of an overseas branch or subsidiary. The result is a restriction on payments to some of the factors of production employed by foreign companies; this restriction is not applicable to local insurers.

The net effect of such restrictions is an extra financing cost imposed on the foreign-owned company. This also applies to restrictions on payments relating to reinsurance cover arranged or provided by the parent organization.

Even where exchange-control regulations allow foreign insurers to remit profits, the existence of unduly stringent rules for valuing assets and/or liabilities for the purpose of assessing a company's solvency may reduce the profits which are available for remittance, especially in an inflationary period. To the extent that more conservative valuation criteria are imposed on foreign insurers, as sometimes occurs, they are clearly discriminatory. But, even when such conservative valuation criteria apply to domestic and foreign insurers equally, they can still discourage foreign supply on account of the deferral of remittable profits.

Discriminatory Capital Requirements
It is a widespread practice for governments to impose minimum capital requirements for locally-incorporated insurance companies. Foreign insurance companies wishing to set up a branch office (as opposed to a subsidiary company) may also be required to deposit a minimum amount of capital.

In other words, governments may treat foreign branches in the same way as locally-established companies, but in so doing they ignore, by differing degrees, the strong legal and financial ties that a branch office has with its overseas parent organization and thus the financial back-up on which policyholders can rely. Generally, levels at which minimum capital, deposit and solvency requirements are set are motivated by a concern for the protection of local policyholders. Sometimes, however, they are aimed at discouraging entry into a market which is deemed to be over-populated.

The size of capital and/or deposit requirements may deter a foreign company from establishing a local organization if, among other things, the existing and expected volume of business does not seem to justify such a capital outlay. As long as the same minimum levels apply to foreign and domestic companies alike, however, they cannot be considered discriminatory. Similarly, even though there may be a misallocation of economic resources resulting from greater fragmentation of reserves, decisions of government authorities to treat a foreign-owned branch in the same way as a foreign-owned subsidiary are not strictly discriminatory.

In a number of markets, however, discrimination does exist in relation to capital and solvency levels.[39] Somewhat paradoxically from the financial viewpoint, such discrimination tends to apply more to branches than to subsidiaries. It may take the form of legislation calling for a larger capital sum to be placed in trust in order to obtain a licence than for a domestic company,[40] or require a stricter enforcement in complying with such capital requirements.[41] Moreover, in some instances, foreign insurers are subject to more stringent solvency criteria than domestic insurers and this will impose a higher capital cost if the volume of business grows.

Discrimination can also arise from an asymmetrical view of overseas-held capital and the free reserves of foreign and domestic insurers. Local supervisory authorities in some countries,[42] while ignoring overseas capital and free reserves of foreign parent organizations as potential cover for local policyholders, nevertheless take into account such capital and free reserves held abroad in respect of the overseas business of domestic insurance companies in assessing their local solvency status.

Local Equity Participation

There has been in recent years a mounting flow of legislation, especially in developing countries, requiring establishment to be through local company status only. As legislation restricting imports of many classes of insurance often exists in these countries, the only way that a foreign insurer can supply insurance services to these markets is by setting up a subsidiary company. While the conversion of an existing branch to local company status is seen by many international insurers as part of an evolutionary development in that the growth of business necessitates greater de-centralization of control, any premature requirement to set up a local company could discourage supply altogether. Indeed, apart from the question of viable size, the political risks associated with deploying extra capital may appear too high.

Such legislation occasionally applies only to new entrants, but, more frequently, it applies to all foreign companies already operating through branches or agencies. Moreover, the conversion must often be effected within a given time period, usually from one to five years. Pressure to domesticate an existing branch can also be achieved through less direct means, in particular by imposing tax penalties on the branches themselves or on their existing and potential customers.

Domestication is often accompanied by legislation requiring some local equity shareholding in foreign-owned subsidiaries. At one extreme, it may be necessary for the foreign parent company to sell only a minority of the issued shares in the company; at the other, the majority of the shares (well over 50 per cent)[43] may have to be sold to local residents, often on disadvantageous terms. In the latter case, foreign insurers either have to supply managerial expertise together with capital over which they have little or no control and on which much of the return is reaped by local interests, or not operate in the country at all. There may be marketing and investment benefits that accrue from having local shareholders,[44] but these are much more likely to be secured through market interaction than by coercion.

Many international insurance companies, while occasionally sharing control in local subsidiaries voluntarily, have generally preferred to hold all of the shares because of management problems associated with joint ownership.[45] Conflict can easily arise over policy issues, such as how much profit is to be ploughed back to finance expansion and how much is to be distributed; when local shareholders are individuals, there tends to be greater pressure to distribute profits and this may have an adverse impact on financing the costs of expansion of the business. In addition, when shares are held by local insurance companies, problems can arise in deciding on appropriate reinsurance arrangements as existing reinsurance may be already integrated into global treaties.

Discriminatory Taxation

The imposition of differential taxes presents a more clear-cut type of discrimination. While there are instances of fiscal discrimination against foreign-owned subsidiaries, more frequently such discrimination is directed at foreign insurers operating through branches. Discriminatory taxes can take the form of higher local tax on profits or higher rates of tax levied on premiums.

Sometimes foreign-owned branches and subsidiaries are not permitted to offset fully against local tax management and other service costs provided by the overseas parent organization.[46] The sum that can be deducted may be limited to either a maximum amount or a maximum percentage of the expenses. In some countries where fire brigades are financed by contributions from local insurance companies, branches of foreign companies may suffer a higher levy on their fire insurance business than domestic companies.

Employment of Non-nationals

To be competitive, it is essential in a service industry such as insurance that adequate management, professional and technical expertise is available to meet local needs. Most international firms in recent years have grown to realize that internal and external benefits can be derived from having nationals in management and other senior positions. Nevertheless, on occasions it is necessary to supplement local management and technical skills by the transfer of personnel, often for a limited period of time, from the parent organization. Indeed, in a service industry the speed of transfer of product and process technology demands a certain degree of labour mobility. The existence of restrictions or delays in obtaining work permits can act as a barrier to the provision of an efficient service, especially in life and corporate insurance, not only in the short term but in the longer term through the loss of on-the-spot training which expatriate staff can provide.

Market Practices

Barriers to successful establishment by a foreign insurance company in a local insurance market can arise from many causes other than government control or policy. Consumer preference for local companies is a natural obstacle which an insurer may seek to overcome by trying to acquire a local identity by, for example, forming or acquiring a local subsidiary, involving local interests, or perhaps operating under a name which does not sound alien.[47] Such measures, however, may not avoid discrimination when seeking to enter a market or even after legal entry.

In some countries foreign insurers are formally excluded from domestic trade associations or their application for membership may encounter opposition from local companies.[48] Such opposition, however, may not always be disadvantageous; indeed, on occasions it may be a positive advantage. For example, membership of a tariff association that requires all member companies to charge the same premium rates and to impose standard policy conditions may prevent a large multinational company from exploiting its advantages.[49] Conversely, if a company's scale of operations in any country is small, forced adherence to low tariff rates may make its operations uneconomic. Alternatively, in certain circumstances, exclusion from membership of a market association may seriously impair a company's competitive position. It may exclude the company from access to vital market information or certain sources of business (such as government contracts) or it may add to operating costs.[50]

Another aspect of the operations of multinational enterprises that has attracted considerable criticism over the last few years is the extent to which bribery has been used to 'smooth the path'. An industry subject to as much official control as insurance is particularly prone to abuses of power on the part of government officials and, although it is difficult to obtain any hard evidence, it is thought that, on occasions, refusal to adhere to local practices on such matters has been followed by administrative difficulties being encountered in obtaining licences and so on.

Finally, as with cross-frontier business, in some countries government procurement rules exclude foreign or foreign-owned insurers from competing for government-controlled insurance.

NOTES AND REFERENCES

1. *International Trade in Services: Insurance: Identification and Analysis of Obstacles, 1983* (Paris: OECD Secretariat, 1983).

2. UNCTAD monitors and records details of changes in the insurance regulations of developing countries in its annual report.

3. For example, in the case of Britain, in order to comply with the requirements of the Road Traffic Acts, 1960-1974, the policy

must be issued by an insurer authorized to carry on motor vehicle insurance business in the European Community and in certain other West European countries.

4. For example, fire insurance of buildings in certain *Länder* in the Federal Republic of Germany and some cantons of Switzerland must be placed with a state-owned insurance organization.

5. For example, France, Italy, Greece, Spain, the Republic of Korea, Libya, Argentina, Brazil, Columbia and South Africa.

6. This practice of fronting is under scrutiny by the governments and supervisory authorities of both developed and developing countries. The State of New York in 1982 issued draft regulations aimed at controlling the 'fronting' of New York risks.

7. Such a situation applies, for example, in Argentina, Brazil, Columbia, Ecuador, Austria, France, Portugal and South Africa. Most states in the United States of America require residents to insure with locally-licensed insurers, with the exception of ocean marine and reinsurance business and surplus-line insurances — that is risks which cannot be placed locally. Surplus-line insurances can be placed either in another state or abroad, but some states apply far more onerous rules than others, including discriminatory taxes on premiums.

8. Imposed by, for example, Argentina, Brazil, Colombia, Dominican Republic, Ecuador, Mexico and Pakistan. In Argentina foreign insurers licensed to write insurance business are not allowed to insure imports.

9. Imposed by, for example, Argentina, Ghana and, in principle, Italy.

10. *Marine Cargo Insurance, op. cit.*

11. Governments that have introduced such measures include Indonesia, Malaysia, Pakistan, Singapore and, amongst the OECD members, Japan and Portugal.

12. *International Trade in Services, op. cit.*

13. Even though formal exchange controls on the remittance abroad of reinsurance premiums are generally far less stringent than the controls applicable to direct premiums, foreign reinsurers often experience considerable delays in obtaining payments from their ceding companies. See for example, *Delay in Settlement of Balances Internationally Resulting from Exchange Control* (London: Reinsurance Offices Association, 1983).

14. For a detailed list of restrictions imposed by most countries, see J.A.S. Neave, 'The Development of Government Involvement

in Reinsurance Underwriting', in *Speaking of Reinsurance...* (Brentford, Middlesex: Kluwer Publishing, 1980).

15. This is the case in Argentina, Brazil, Egypt, Italy, Japan, Kenya and Nigeria.

16. In other words, to transfer to a reinsurance company.

17. A reinsurer will transfer part of the risk he has accepted to another reinsurer under a retrocession contract.

18. For example, in Argentina:

(a) national companies are obliged to cede to the Instituto Nacional de Reaseguros (INDER) the excess of their retention up to the limit of the automatic cover granted by the Institute;

(b) national companies can cede four times their net retentions with other national companies before ceding to INDER under treaties, copies of which must be lodged with the Superintendent of Insurance; and

(c) foreign companies and local companies with foreign participation in the capital must cede 30 per cent of the premium income at the original terms of acquisition, 30 per cent must be ceded to INDER or national companies at terms to be agreed upon and 40 per cent can be freely disposed of.

19. For example, African insurers have to make compulsory cessions to the African Reinsurance Corporation.

20. These are reciprocal inter-governmental agreements whereby tax levied locally on overseas income can be offset against a company's tax liability in its country of domicile. For example, income tax payable in the United States by a British company's American subsidiary can be offset against the parent company's tax liability in the United Kingdom.

21. In the United States the federal excise tax on direct insurances is only 4 per cent of premiums and only 1 per cent for reinsurances.

22. In Austria the premium tax on insurances placed with foreign non-admitted insurers may be five times higher than on insurances written by domestic companies unless the risk cannot be covered locally.

23. Ireland, Trinidad and Venezuela afford instances of such tax discrimination.

24. This form of discrimination is used, for example, in Malaysia.

25. Australia and New Zealand operate such policies.

26. Such 'gross reserving' regulations are to be found in most states in the United States and in a few continental European countries. Banks, led by Citibank and Bank of America, have been

prepared to supply financial guarantees (that is, letters of credit) to minimize the capital costs associated with these gross reserving regulations. Even though the financial guarantees supplied by banks reduce these capital costs since ceding insurers do not have to carry additional assets, they are not supplied free. See Carter and Dickinson, 'Economic Effects of Restrictions on International Trade in Reinsurance', Proceedings, 3rd International Reinsurances Conference, Reinsurance Offices Association, Cambridge, 1977.

27. It might be argued that in relatively free and efficient international capital and foreign-exchange markets, no 'strong' currencies exist. But this is not true for tax-paying insurers and reinsurers because of the asymmetric tax treatment of unrealized currency gains and interest rates, the former being free of tax. Hence relatively strong currencies tend to be those with low interest rates since exchange rates and interest rates are jointly determined in international markets where tax effects are minimal.

28. Neave, 'The Effect on International Reinsurance of Changing Patterns in Economic Relationships', in *Speaking of Reinsurance...*, *op. cit.*

29. This is the case in Denmark, Finland, France, Greece, Italy, Japan, New Zealand, Portugal, Sweden, Malaysia, the Philippines and Singapore and, other than for marine insurances, the Federal Republic of Germany and Norway.

30. The right of the German supervisory authority to apply these regulations to business placed with insurers authorized to write the business in other member countries has been challenged by the Commission as infringing the provisions of the Treaty of Rome.

31. *International Trade in Services*, *op. cit.*, p. 10.

32. The most extensive scheme has been established in New Zealand providing a comprehensive compensation scheme for persons in employment for injuries sustained by any type of accident.

33. For example, this has been the case in Algeria, Burma, Costa Rica, Egypt, Ethiopia, India, Iraq, Syria, Seychelles, Tanzania and Zambia, though Zambia is now denationalizing.

34. For example, the establishment directives of the European Community provide for insurers to be given authorization to write only specified classes of insurance and for no new companies to be licensed to write both long-term (life) and general insurance business.

35. It is notable that Japan, for example, where foreign insurers control only about 2.5 per cent of non-life premiums and a minute

amount of life insurance, had until the mid-1970s issued few licences to foreign insurance companies. Since that time Japanese authorities have allowed a number of foreign insurance companies to enter the Japanese market. This is an improvement, but only time will tell whether or not these foreign insurance companies can secure a significant market share. The issue of delays in gaining admission to insurance markets in developed economies has also been recognized by Ripoll, 'UNCTAD and Insurance', *op. cit.*, p. 84.

36. This has occurred in Ghana, Mexico, Nigeria, Venezuela and Peru.

37. Examples of this type of legislation can be found in Argentina, Bolivia, Colombia, Ecuador, Mexico, Morocco, Uganda, Thailand, the Dominican Republic, Peru, Turkey and Venezuela. Malaysia is also proceeding towards a situation where nationals hold at least 70 per cent of the shares in all insurance companies and have majority representation on the board of directors.

38. Such is often the case in a number of countries in Africa, the Far East and in South America.

39. Jordan, Kuwait and the United Arab Emirates require foreign-owned companies to have higher minimum paid-up capital than locally-owned insurers.

40. This is the case, for example, in the Dominican Republic, Malaysia and Sierra Leone.

41. In Japan, when foreign insurers are able to obtain a licence, they are required to furnish a substantial capital deposit; domestic companies, although they may be required to deposit a similar amount, are rarely required to do so.

42. Including Portugal, Greece and Cyprus.

43. In Chile, Colombia, Ecuador, Peru and Venezuela 80 per cent of the shares in local companies must be held by citizens or residents and no new investment by overseas companies will be allowed.

44. After the Royal Insurance Company had sold a proportion of its shareholding in its Venezuelan company to local residents in 1976, the chairman of the company said that the wider local shareholding had had a substantial influence on the amount of business which the company obtained.

45. Maurice Greenberg, President of the American International Group, has said that where his company's share had been forced below 50 per cent and management changes had been imposed, standards had been lowered and corporate objectives changed

invariably for the worse. 'International Problems and Possible Solutions', paper presented to the International Insurance Seminar, San Francisco, 1976.

46. Such tax regulations apply in Norway, Morocco, Pakistan and South Africa.

47. Nationale Nederlanden, one of the world's major insurance groups, has pursued an aggressive policy of international expansion since the mid-1960s by purchasing indigenous insurance companies and retaining the names of the companies acquired. See Dickinson and W. Zadjlic, *Changing International Insurance Markets: their Implications for EEC Insurance Enterprises and Governments* (Brussels: Centre for European Policy Studies, 1986).

48. In Japan foreign insurers are excluded from the Marine and Fire Insurance Association: see Ripoll, 'UNCTAD and Insurance', *op. cit.*, who quotes allegations published in *The Economist*, London, 12 February 1972.

49. Not surprisingly, support for the continuation of tariffs in fire insurance in Britain came from non-tariff companies who were free to compete in whatever manner they choose. Carter and Neil Doherty, 'Tariff Control and the Public Interest', *Journal of Risk and Insurance*, Bloomington, Illinois, September 1974.

50. Membership, for example, of the Institute of London Underwriters gives a company access to its policy signing and accounting services which considerably simplify dealings with brokers.

Chapter 5

Analysis of the Effects of Discriminatory Measures

THE PREVIOUS chapter outlined the restrictions imposed on international transactions in insurance and reinsurance. In this chapter the effects of those measures on the countries imposing them are analyzed with respect to

(a) domestic consumers of insurance services,

(b) the economy as a whole and

(c) the balance of payments.

The global economic effects of barriers to international trade in insurance will also be examined briefly.

Effects on Local Consumers of Insurance Provision

The extent to which the absence or reduced level of foreign supply of insurance services will affect consumer satisfaction depends on the circumstances existing in a particular market. The general conditions which would determine consumer welfare are:

(a) the degree and level of sophistication of local needs;

(b) the extent to which local insurers are capable of supplying those needs efficiently; and

(c) the efficiency of foreign insurers capable and, in the absence of any restrictions, willing to supply those needs.

The extent of the loss of consumer welfare flowing from discriminatory measures will vary according to the type of insurance required and whether restrictions affect the establishment of, or export of insurance services by, foreign insurers.

Consumer Choice

The obstacles to insurers selling direct insurances across frontiers will be dealt with first. As a general rule the inability to buy from an insurer not licensed to transact business within the country (a non-admitted insurer) is not likely to affect seriously the choice of individuals and small firms, especially in the case of life insurance. The needs of such consumers tend to be relatively unsophisticated, but more important, as argued in Chapter 3, most individuals are reluctant to deal with companies which do not have a local organization. Nevertheless, there are instances, particularly in connection with overseas trade and travel, where small firms and individuals may need more extensive cover than is available in their local market.

The insurance needs of large organizations, on the other hand, are far more complex and require more flexible insurance contracts than a local market may be able or willing to supply.[1] Technological and other developments create demands for new types of risks requiring highly specialized knowledge and underwriting skill which is only available in sophisticated markets. Consequently, restrictions on access to international insurance markets can significantly reduce available choice for large industrial and commercial buyers of insurance.

Restrictions on either establishment of foreign insurers or on the freedom of licensed companies to provide the insurances they are willing to supply may seriously impair the range of insurance provision for all consumers. Usually the type of foreign insurance company that tends to establish abroad, given a conducive environment, is the multinational group with experience of producing a wide range of services and products in other markets, including some where product development is an important part of the competitive process. It includes not only the devising of new forms of insurance to cater for new risks and the adapting of existing insurance contracts to meet changing consumer requirements, but also the packaging of existing products in new ways in order to reduce sales and administrative costs and provide the consumer with contracts that give wider cover at lower costs. Some of the new packages that have been devised in recent years by insurers seeking to expand their market shares have also included insurance against additional risks and/or other services or have incorporated more flexible terms to meet consumers' changing needs. Not only do consumers benefit from the introduction of such products and services but also the market as a whole tends to gain. If new ideas imported into a market by a foreign insurer prove successful they can be copied quickly by local companies because there are no patent laws relating to insurance services.

It has been argued that multinational insurers in some markets have tended to introduce policies which, while they embody new developments, do not suit particular needs; alternatively, it has been said that they concentrate their sales efforts on one segment of the market.[2] This has been advanced as a reason in some developing countries for not allowing foreign insurers to compete. Even if this were true, although the supporting evidence is far from strong, it does not necessarily follow that the presence in a market of foreign insurers will mean the range of policies on offer will generally be unsuited to local needs. Such a situation could occur only if:

(a) all established foreign insurers collectively agreed, either expressly or tacitly, on the types of insurances to be made available;

(b) they have a monopoly or can so influence local companies that they offer no effective competition; and

(c) there is no potential competition from new entrants.

Such a set of conditions would be unlikely to persist in an open market. Perception of a substantial local need for insurance for which there is an effective and unsatisfied demand would present an innovator, whether local or foreign, with an important new source of business.[3]

Quality of Service

Restrictions on insuring domestic risks abroad are usually of no great consequence to the smaller buyers of insurance since it is generally recognized that a local presence constitutes an integral aspect of the quality of service provided by an insurer.[4] The provision of local services by local agents, brokers and loss adjusters to complement such cross-frontier business, even if permitted, is unlikely to match that that can be provided by established local insurers, at least for standard insurance products.

Purely domestic insurers, however, cannot match the service which the large multinational insurance enterprises, Lloyd's and major brokers can provide for international risks, particularly in relation to the insurance of liability for goods and services produced and/or sold internationally and for marine, aviation and other international transport risks. A prerequisite of an efficient service is access to a worldwide network capable of inspecting and assessing loss where it occurs together with the possession of ancillary legal and banking services to facilitate the prompt payment of claims. Local insurers, including state monopolies, are often unlikely to have easy access to such a worldwide facility. Even where foreign insurers have been allowed to establish locally, they may not be able to offer as good an international service because of local regulations on premiums, policy coverages *et cetera* as Lloyd's or other insurance companies which, for various reasons, are willing to provide cover only on a cross-frontier basis. As well as reducing consumer choice, limitations on the placing abroad of insurances for imports or exports generally interferes with, and may add to the costs of, international trade.[5]

In the case of the prohibition or discouragement of establishment by foreign insurers, the losses in quality of service are likely to be greater for large corporations, including government-owned enterprises, than for individuals and small business. The large multinational insurance enterprises that seek to establish abroad are, because of their size and easier access to international reinsurance and capital markets, often in a better position to provide cover for high risks which arise either from natural hazards or from risk concentrations found in large-scale, technologically-advanced industrial processes and transport vehicles. Moreover, they possess an important advantage over the purely nationally-based company in supplying cover for large-scale industrial and commercial risks. By underwriting similar risks elsewhere in the world, they can build up the statistical data and the technical competence to estimate possible loss frequencies and loss severities.[6] Local insurers in a protected market would not normally possess a credible set of data to price such cover, at least not to the satisfaction of the international reinsurance market on which they would need to depend.

In recent years, corporate buyers of insurance in many markets have not only demanded extensive and flexible policies but also a range of supporting services such as loss prevention, engineering and risk management advice. Again, it has tended to be the large insurers and reinsurers operating in advanced competitive markets that have pioneered such services and have built up internal resources which can be made available to corporate consumers on a worldwide basis. The major international brokers have also developed similar supporting services, however, which sometimes can be supplied in markets that inhibit entry to foreign insurers.

Although in relation to the quality of service available to domestic policyholders, barriers to international trade in direct insurance are undoubtedly more important than restrictions on the access of domestic companies to international reinsurance markets, the latter should not be ignored. The major reinsurance companies have developed important technical services which are available to their ceding insurers. For example, they can provide assistance in the investigation of causes of loss, in the salvaging of property and the rehabilitation of business and injured persons after losses have occurred. This benefits both insurers and their policyholders.

Level and Stability of Insurance Prices

Foreign insurers have variously been accused both of making excessive profits, particularly in developing countries, and of temporarily destabilizing insurance markets by driving down premiums to uneconomic levels. Even if such accusations are correct, neither situation is a sufficient ground for excluding foreign insurers from a national market. As Brian Hindley, of the Trade Policy Research Centre in London, argues, one explanation for high profits may be that foreign insurers are more efficient than local companies.[7] The interests of policyholders would then best be served by encouraging further entry to the market to intensify the competitive pressures on premium rates. The exclusion of foreign insurers to enable premium rates to rise sufficiently to support relatively inefficient local companies would simply benefit local producers at the expense of consumers.

Clearly the influence of foreign insurers on market prices and their impact on policyholder welfare is not clear-cut. It is necessary to recognize the interdependence of price and quality of service; the provision of a higher quality service increases costs, whether the increase in quality is due to wider cover or to the provision of ancillary services, such as loss prevention advice. Thus it is possible that foreign suppliers of insurance, if they were allowed to enter a previously protected market, might have a higher price structure than companies already established and yet be fully competitive by virtue of offering a higher quality service.[8] Price, therefore, refers to a given quality of service and low quality/price ratios are a feature of many developing countries.[9]

The presence of a foreign supplier on a market might result in lower prices if the costs of providing and marketing its services were lower than those of local insurers. This can arise if the foreign insurer:

(a) is able to acquire factor inputs — risk capital, skilled labour, technology and reinsurance — at a lower cost than local suppliers;

(b) has developed more efficient operational and marketing systems;

(c) is able to exploit any increasing returns to scale (including the smaller variability of claims costs associated with the combining of an insurer's world-wide business into large diversified insurance portfolios) to a greater degree than local producers;[10] or

(d) enjoys lower corporate taxation and/or regulatory restrictions.

Of course, even if such cost advantages do exist, it cannot necessarily be inferred that they invariably lead to lower market prices. There are examples, however, where international competition has had such an effect.[11] There may be others, however, which point to the opposite — it would require a major research effort to produce conclusive evidence either way. It is necessary to look, therefore, at the conditions prevailing in insurance markets and to analyze the probable effects.

First, it should be recognized that, because of certain differences in the mix of factor inputs, business acquisition costs, scales of production and tax structures,[12] the supply of foreign insurance on a cross-frontier basis is likely to result in a cost structure different from that of local supply. On the other hand, because of unavoidable fixed costs, the initial production costs of a new entrant setting up a local subsidiary or branch office will tend to be relatively high until it reaches a viable size, although that problem may be avoided if entry is secured by way of taking over an existing local company. A foreign insurer exporting services to a foreign market avoids the capital costs involved in establishment. Consequently, as far as new entrants are concerned, barriers to cross-frontier insurance business will in some situations be more likely to result in greater potential losses to consumers, at least in the short term, than barriers to establishment.

Economic theory does not predict with certainty the long-run effects on market prices of a government permitting new entry to an imperfectly competitive market. Consequently, the result of the removal of obstacles to cross-frontier insurance business and to establishment of foreign insurers is uncertain. Obviously local companies would be exposed to additional potential competition which would tend to make them more price conscious,[13] but the final effect in any particular market would depend upon:

(a) the existing market structure, conditions and behaviour of insurers already established in the market; and

(b) the possible existence and size of other barriers.

The more inefficient local insurers are and/or the higher the premium rates they are able to charge as a result of their protected position, the greater the attractions of the market to foreign insurers. The potential reductions in market premium rates would be greater after the entry of foreign insurers, provided they were not inhibited by other barriers.

Inadequate competition in insurance markets often leads to a good deal of cross-subsidization among consumers. Policyholders in lower risk classes may not receive adequate price compensation for their lower loss propensities[14] and small to medium-sized corporate buyers may have to pay relatively more than large buyers who can exercise counter-vailing power through their ability to opt for a higher degree of self-insurance if they consider the cost of conventional insurance too high.[15] If foreign companies bring to the market superior technical competence in discriminating between risk classes, less cross-subsidization would probably follow.[16]

Minimum prices for certain classes of cover are sometimes set by tariff organizations; transportation and life insurances and reinsurances are normally excluded. The motivation behind the formation of these organizations and their support by governments, rests on attempts to prevent prices falling to levels which might endanger the solvency of insurers as well as to ensure greater stability of the supply of insurance cover

over time. To the extent that these minimum-price structures are based on the average costs of local insurers and on prevailing underwriting and marketing methods, as is often the case, the opportunity for foreign sources of supply to pass on any reduction of costs from more efficient provision in the form of lower premiums could well be circumscribed in the short term. In the longer term, of course, foreign insurers could expect to increase their market share; indeed, the presence of foreign insurers in some markets has reduced the rigidity of local tariff organizations.[17]

In certain conditions, however, it is possible that the introduction to a protected market of foreign sources of supply might exert upward pressures on the level of prices for certain classes of business. Such a situation could exist if the market was already serviced by a state monopoly or a group of local insurers who were exploiting increasing returns to scale within the market. The introduction of foreign sources of supply might lead to a fragmentation of the local market and result in higher costs and hence higher prices.

Although there may be markets where the presence of a large number of local and foreign insurers raises costs and so prices all round, there are reasons for discounting the possibility of any substantial losses resulting from opening a market to the new entry of foreign insurers, notably:

(a) available evidence indicates that the economies of scale, of which insurance companies can take advatage, are relatively small;[18] and

(b) low market premium rates would be a disincentive to foreign companies deciding whether to enter the market.

It is possible, however, that the entry of foreign companies, particularly through the establishment of local branch offices or subsidiaries, might lead to higher prices because of rigidities in the prevailing marketing system. For example, if agents and brokers have a strong grip on a market, they may be able to extract higher commission rates from the increased number of companies competing for business, particularly if the public is unaware of price differentials between companies. On the other hand, the response of some insurers may be to develop new methods of marketing their products through direct selling or the use of exclusive agents, passing on the benefits of the lower costs to policyholders through lower premium rates. In any event, it is illogical for a government to discriminate against foreign insurers when setting conditions for new entrants, since a large established company may be prepared to subsidize its operations until the market has expanded sufficiently to provide it with an adequate operating base. In addition, it is more likely to fulfil a beneficial innovatory role than an inexperienced, newly-established local company.

The discussion so far has been centred on the total exclusion of foreign insurers from a domestic market. More frequently, discriminatory measures simply impair the relative ability of foreign insurers to compete with local companies. Virtually all types of government restrictions and taxation result, in differing degrees, in higher costs. When such restrictions discriminate against foreign suppliers of insurance services they reduce, and may more than offset, any relative cost advantage which the foreign supplier may possess. Consequently, the existence of such discriminatory restrictions may lead to higher market prices, either directly or indirectly, through a reduction in competition.

Some measures, while not discriminatory in that they are not deliberately applied to distort relative efficiencies, nevertheless do so because of their greater impact on foreign insurers. Policies aimed at the 'localization' of premium balances and reserve funds may be neutral in intent, but frequently they result in distortion. Conceptually, the degree of this distortion may be measured by the difference between the level of funds required to be held locally and the level which an efficient insurer, following a prudent policy of currency matching, would otherwise have chosen. While it is difficult to generalize, two situations may be distinguished:

    (a) Apart from restrictions on the remittance of profits
to parent companies, the 'localization' of funds arising

from life insurance operations of local branches and subsidiaries of foreign insurers should not normally cause much, if any, distortion, provided the valuation basis used to determine local solvency requirements is not unduly conservative and inflexible;

(b) In the case of insurances and reinsurances arranged on a cross-frontier basis and non-life insurances arranged through locally established branches or subsidiaries, the localization of premium balances is likely to increase a foreign insurance company's operating costs, particularly if the regulations extend to reserve funds in excess of expected local claims costs, because part of its capital will effectively be frozen.[19] The more widespread are such practices, the more debilitating the effect. Thus the international insurer will, for a given underwriting portfolio and a given probability of financial ruin, have to maintain more capital or higher levels of reinsurance than otherwise would be required.

Reference has been made already to the special position of reinsurers. Stringent deposit requirements run counter to the risk reduction advantages obtained from writing a geographically well-diversified reinsurance portfolio. This fact has been recognized by the European Community which, in providing full freedom for international reinsurance transactions as the first step in its insurance programme, did not impose any localization-of-reserves requirements on non-Community reinsurers.

The extra costs to the foreign insurance company of acquiring and maintaining additional capital or a higher level of reinsurance will tend to be passed on to the final consumer.[20] The degree to which the extra cost is transferred to local consumers, however, will depend on the way in which the costs of the parent company are allocated. Moreover, the costs will be even higher if reinsurers supplying cover to the foreign insurer are themselves subject to a 'localization' constraint. Indeed, when foreign suppliers of reinsurance are subject to 'localization' restrictions on premium balances, either directly or as a result of 'gross reserving', not only will foreign insurers be affected but local companies and reinsurers relying on external cover will be affected too.

Likewise, restrictions on work permits for foreigners may add to operating costs of locally-established foreign companies. One of their major advantages is access to highly trained expatriate staff and, if they are forced to hand over the running of their operation to less skilled people, efficiency will inevitably decline and operating costs rise. If sufficient suitably trained people are available locally, it will generally be cheaper to employ them and, likewise, a company will have a longer-term interest in providing training facilities. But the costs, to policyholders of forcing out expatriate employees could be high.[21]

Meeting Financial Obligations

Insofar as foreign insurers are better managed, possess larger capital, write a geographically wider-spread business and have easier access to international reinsurance and capital markets than domestic companies, they can offer a higher degree of security for policyholders. By the same token, less efficient and financially weaker insurers will not.

In either event it can be argued that it is in the local consumer's interest that foreign suppliers of insurance and reinsurance should be screened and monitored to the same degree as local companies. Local foreign-owned subsidiary companies create no particular supervisory problems. The difficulties arise where the security available for local policyholders is dependent upon the global activities and financial state of a foreign insurer. This would be the case where a company operates through local branch offices or particularly where it supplies insurances on a cross-frontier basis so that the company has no local presence and is thus outside the jurisdiction of the local supervisory authority. The issue may be further complicated when governments in other countries require the localization of funds so that the assets available to meet the claims of other policyholders are diminished.

A government can, of course, make the supply of insurance and reinsurance services conditional on foreign companies submitting to an investigation of their global solvency positions to ensure that they meet a prescribed standard of solvency. The implementation of such measures, however, raises severe practical problems besides being very costly for all parties. Moreover, it provides no guarantee that if the company should run into financial difficulties funds will be available to meet the liabilities to local policyholders.[22]

Consequently, governments tend to adopt the simpler solution of requiring all foreign companies either to operate as locally-registered subsidiary companies or to maintain funds locally. Mention has already been made of the resulting cost to policyholders and the adverse effect on an insurance company's global financial strength caused by any fragmentation of its capital funds. Moreover, in a rapidly changing economic and social environment, it has not only become increasingly difficult to forecast the capital required to finance operations in any one country but also to guarantee that additional capital can readily be obtained if and when required. Thus the ability of the large multinational insurance company to move funds internationally is increasingly advantageous from the standpoint of financial stability.

A better solution to the problem would be for governments to agree on minimum standards of solvency for insurance companies and to rely on enforcement by the supervisory authority in the home country of each international enterprise. There will be more discussion on this in Chapter 8.

Agreement on these matters will not be easy to achieve, as European experience demonstrates. Not only do ideas differ regarding solvency regulation but also in many countries accounting and insurance supervisory standards leave much to be desired. As the UNCTAD Secretariat has admitted:

'...Third World insurance markets operate at present according to up-to-date insurance legislation. How well these legislations are implemented in practice is a different matter; there seem to be some serious problems, due to a certain lack of sufficient political support of insurance supervision on the part of the ministries responsible for it, as well as lack of adequate insurance training of the staff of the supervisory authorities.

'Bearing in mind the importance to the insured public and to the national economy in general of effective insurance supervision, more efforts should be made to remedy the above situation prevailing in many countries.'[23]

Therefore to be realistic, such a solution may be feasible in the first instance only in respect of insurance transactions between industrialized countries.

Finally, there is the possibility of foreign competition forcing down market prices and so undermining the solvency of weaker local companies. Insofar as the threat to local insurers results from unfair competition, most governments possess powers to deal with such behaviour. If, however, it flows from the greater efficiency of foreign companies, then the controlled winding-up of inefficient local companies may be accepted as a short-term cost which in the longer term will be more than offset by the benefit which policyholders gain from a more efficient insurance industry.

EFFECTS ON THE NATIONAL ECONOMY

Although restrictions on foreign suppliers of insurance may be seen to result usually in a welfare loss for policyholders, it is possible that discrimination may still be justifiable from a wider economic standpoint. The effect on the economies of countries imposing barriers to trade in insurance services will now be discussed. A detailed analysis of the economic effects would require an attempt to trace and measure the impact of the existence of these barriers on real output or, more generally, on the national economic objectives of individual countries. Because of the relative size of the insurance industry *vis-à-vis* the rest of the economy and because of the limited scope of this essay, the analysis here will be rather general.

Efficient Allocation of Resources

A useful starting point is to outline those resources which are consumed in providing insurance and reinsurance, both of which require much the same inputs. Being a service, the provision of insurance is a labour-intensive activity demanding a well-educated labour force and a wide range of professional expertise in financial, legal and technical subjects.[24] Capital is required for office accommodation, to set up office equipment (including computer facilities) and to train staff. The major part of the capital requirement, however, is for relatively liquid or marketable funds to act as a cushion against uncertain claims costs. While the insurance industry is not a high-technology industry, it demands a good degree of financial and marketing expertise. The quality and intensity of resource utilization varies significantly with the type of insurance; the provision of personal insurance services demands a lower capital, skilled-labour and technological input than the provision of corporate or transportation insurance services. Similarly, because of its international and wholesaling character, reinsurance requires a more sophisticated labour and technological input and greater capital support than direct insurance.[25]

Barriers to foreign sources of supply may affect the quantity of domestically-owned resources employed in the provision of insurance services. It is possible that the expulsion of foreign insurers may merely remove surplus supply from the domestic direct insurance and/or reinsurance market if the market shares of the foreign insurers can be taken up by local domestically-owned insurers who can then operate at full capacity. In any other circumstances, unless the local domestically-owned companies employ the resources released by the withdrawal of foreign insurers then the provision of insurance services will decline.

It would be foolish to assert that the efficiency of any industry is invariably inversely related to the degree of protection it is given against foreign competition. Such protection, however, does blunt the spur which would encourage local companies to employ resources as efficiently as possible in order to avoid losing business to foreign suppliers. Also it is possible that losses to the economy resulting from protection may be justified if protection enables a local industry to develop to the point where it can yield long-term social benefits greater than the short-term losses.[26]

Viewed from the standpoint of the whole economy, rather than from the sectional interest of policyholders, the case for lowering the barriers to international transactions in insurance revolves around the alternative use of domestically-owned resources which are no longer needed to provide insurance services because of the existence of a supply of foreign insurance. The crucial question is whether such resources can be used more productively elsewhere in the economy. There is no clear answer to this question[27] since it depends on where, and how quickly, the resources could be deployed. Unfortunately, restrictions on insurance trade are often part of a panoply of restrictions forming the general policy of import protection and, consequently, there is no guarantee that the capital, labour and entrepreneurial skills released will be used in the production of goods or services in which the country may have a greater comparative advantage.

The argument for imposing restrictions on the foreign supply of insurance services is frequently based on the existence of unemployed or under-utilized labour, particularly in developing countries. Since the insurance industry is labour-intensive and does not place the same demands on capital resources that many other industries do, such an argument might seem to have some force as far as cross-frontier insurance business is concerned. All arguments, however, which seek to put employment considerations ahead of efficiency in the allocation of resources can be shown, from the normative economic standpoint, to be no better than second-best short-term solutions.[28]

Acquisition of Insurance Expertise

Closely related to the question of employment of local labour is the suggestion that the provision of insurance by foreign companies impedes the acquisition of insurance expertise by residents and thereby inhibits the development of a local insurance industry. The issue is of particular importance to developing countries with newly-established insurance industries.

It is possible, of course, for a national market to be controlled entirely by foreign insurers and for all the insurance needs of residents to be met either through cross-frontier transactions or through local establishments wholly staffed by expatriates. Clearly in these circumstances it would be difficult for residents to acquire the expertise required to manage and run an insurance company.

Nowhere, however, does such a situation exist. Foreign insurers admitted to a market find it more efficient to employ and train local staff for most of their sales and administrative tasks even if, at least initially, they reserve senior appointments for expatriates.[29] It is then impossible to prevent local insurers from poaching staff who are likely to have been trained in the best market practices and to high technical standards. Thus the establishment of foreign insurers is more likely to foster rather than hinder the acquisition of the latest insurance expertise by the residents of a country. There are also many opportunities in various worldwide centres for overseas students to obtain education and training in insurance.

The supply of insurance from abroad, or the presence of foreign insurers on a local market, may slow down the rate of development of a nationally-owned industry. Nevertheless, the evidence indicates that, without any assistance from government, locally-owned and managed insurers can become established, can compete against established foreign companies and can acquire an increasing share of the market.[30]

Thus Professor Brian Hindley has concluded that for developing countries (and his conclusions must carry even greater weight for developed countries), the argument that the presence of foreign insurers impedes residents in acquiring insurance skills

'...carries very little weight as a guide to policy in developing countries. There is a strong case for government to facilitate the acquisition of skills by its constituents, but this is a quite general case, involving policy towards education. Formal education in insurance matters might well be included in such a policy, but the infancy of the insurance industry does not provide good grounds for any other intervention'.[31]

Indirect Effects of Restrictions on Supply

In the above discussion there has been an implicit assumption that restrictions on foreign sources of supply do not significantly affect the level or quality of insurance services supplied even though they may lead to a relatively inefficient use of resources. If, however, the supply of insurance cover is adversely affected, this may have important economic effects because insurance is itself an input in the production of other goods and services in an economy. Indirect effects may have a greater impact than direct effects in two ways.

First, the lack of insurance cover could result in a reduction in the risk-taking propensity of businessmen which, in turn, could lead to a reduction in output and employment. Even if more risky investment decisions are not deferred, output and employment could still suffer if firms decide to carry a higher level of working capital to cover the extra operating risks. Moreover, the absence of an adequate supply of property and liability insurance for new, technologically-advanced products and processes may adversely affect the growth potential in some countries. Large multinational enterprises which may have both the capital and the type of technology needed in some countries may be deterred from setting up a business in a country where there is no adequate insurance cover. They may also fear that discriminatory measures may be applied to them.

Inadequate insurance may also adversely affect the general level of trade in various ways. For example, a country's exports may suffer if a government insists that transportation insurance has to be arranged through a local insurer in whom the importers in other countries have little confidence. Likewise, any reduction in the quantity or quality of loss-prevention advice provided by insurers would probably be followed by a rise in losses of, or damage to, economic resources which might then reduce the levels of output and employment.

Second, local capital funds may prove to be an inadequate substitute for the capital resources available to international insurers. Where the productive capacity of a country is concentrated either in a few small areas exposed to natural disasters such as earthquakes, or in a relatively few, very large productive units subject to the risks associated with high technology, the occurrence of a disaster could have a calamitous effect on the economy and leave both the insured properties and local insurers' funds in ruins.[32] The enforced localization of funds or premium balances of foreign insurers and reinsurers presents the same sort of danger. Government policy decisions relating to the prohibition or restriction of foreign supplies of insurance often appear to disregard these indirect effects when they could be the most important considerations of all.

Mobilization and Investment of
   Capital Funds
As already explained, insurance companies do not simply provide insurance services; they are also involved in the mobilization and allocation of capital funds. In particular, life insurers can, and in many countries do, play an important role in mobilizing the small savings of individuals and channelling them into long-term investment in the private or public sectors.[33] This mobilization role can be important, not

only in developing countries where there is acute shortage of capital but also in developed economies, where it could help to counter the tendency for the average propensity to consume to increase with the narrowing of income differentials.

Cross-frontier personal life insurance business is negligible and is likely to remain so until modern communications technology becomes widespread. Any restrictions on the cross-frontier provision of life insurance, therefore, would have only limited effects on the mobilization of personal savings in an economy.

The counterpart to the mobilization of funds is their investment. Naturally most if not all governments want to see funds flowing to local capital markets in view of the important role they play in economic development. But any interference with the freedom of insurers, whether foreign or locally-owned, to invest their funds how and where they consider appropriate in the light of prevailing conditions may run counter to the interests of policyholders and, in extreme cases, to the long-run national economic interest too.

For example, if insurance companies are required to invest more of their funds in government securities than seems prudent to them, this would have two main effects.

(a) Policyholders may get a lower return on their savings:

(b) Funds which the insurance companies are required to channel into government securities may be used to finance current public consumption — in other words, to meet short-term goals. This could have adverse effects on the growth of the economy.

Life insurance companies, as a rule, have long investment horizons simply because of the nature of their liabilities; they are increasingly interested in equity investments because the return on equities is expected at least to keep pace with inflation, thus enabling insurance companies to maintain the real value of the savings of their policyholders.

Of course, as Professor Hindley points out in his analysis

of the effects of restrictions by developing countries on insurance companies investing funds abroad, there is always the possibility that insurance companies if left to their own devices may make decisions, which are not in the best interests of local policyholders. For example, they may overlook or seriously under-estimate the returns available from investing in a particular country. That is not a sound reason, however, for discriminating against foreign insurers on the grounds that they are more likely wrongly to transfer funds abroad than local insurers. Even if this proved to be the case there could be two equally rational explanations. The first is that in comparison with foreign insurers, local insurers might be less efficient and/or more willing to sacrifice the interests of their policyholders for patriotic reasons. The second is that the foreign insurers may be more likely to under-estimate potential investment yields because they do not have the same information as local insurers. In such a case they would be at a competitive disadvantage in competing against local insurers for business. They would, in these circumstances, have every incentive to hire local residents to acquire access to the same sources of information and investment expertise.[34]

BALANCE-OF-PAYMENTS EFFECTS

Balance-of-payments considerations have been a major factor in the erection of barriers to international insurance transactions and, in particular, to cross-frontier business. While countries will be influenced by their own international competitive position in assessing balance-of-payments considerations, the issue is inevitably bound up with the nature of the existing international monetary system and the general level of confidence in this system. Because of the self-regulating mechanism implicit in a system of floating exchange rates, balance-of-payments considerations should now prove to be less inhibiting than under the fixed exchange-rate system which prevailed during most of the post-World War II period.[35]

Whether a system of fixed or floating exchange rates is assumed, there is no single analytical model which can be adopted to assess, with certainty, the balance-of-payments effects across different economies. The discussion that follows, therefore, will be set out in general terms. The effects will be examined from the viewpoint of the financing of government deficits, since it has tended to be shortages of foreign-currency holdings that have been a major economic motive behind the erection of some of the barriers to insurance trade and establishment. First, there will be a look at the direct balance-of-payments effects[36] and then at the indirect effects, including those on consumers of insurance services.

In the absence of any restrictions, the supply of insurance by foreign insurers would most likely affect the balance-of-payments in the following ways.

Cross-frontier Business

The import of insurance and reinsurance results first of all in a premium outflow which is normally financed through the foreign-exchange market, followed in time by a countervailing inflow of claims payments. The average time-lag between the two flows will vary with the type of insurance and the growth rate of the portfolio. For example, non-life reinsurance usually has a longer lag than direct non-life insurance and liability insurances have a longer lag than property insurances. The longer the time-lag, or the faster the growth rate of the portfolio, the smaller will be the reduction in the cost to the balance of payments in a given year provided by the inflow of claims payments.

When exchange controls exist, but outward premium flows are permitted, it is not uncommon to find that insurers and reinsurers experience delays in obtaining the requisite foreign exchange from the monetary authorities. In recent years, these delays have lengthened in many developing countries as foreign-exchange reserves have been low and it has been difficult to replenish them through further borrowing. In practice, delays are more of a problem in reinsurance since permission to import insurance directly is rarely given in some developing countries. Claim outflows can also be subject to delay. The existence of these delays can alter the time pattern of the cash flows and hence can reduce the balance-of-payments costs of external reinsurance. Reinsurers, of course, may raise premiums to compensate for expected delays by ceding companies in remitting balances and, if they do, it will have a counter effect on the balance-of-payments position.

Insurers and reinsurers operating internationally have an obligation to pay claims whenever, wherever and in whatever currency they arise. Consequently, they have a general preference for currency matching.[37] Funds obtained from prepayments of premiums will usually be retained for investment in the financial assets of the country of operation if the volume of business warrants it and if local markets and exchange-control conditions are satisfactory. If this happens the potential balance-of-payments cost of external insurance and reinsurance will be reduced. Relatively few developing countries, however, possess the sophisticated capital and money markets insurance companies require, so they are less likely to attract portfolio investment inflows than developed countries, except where there are strong marketing reasons for doing so.[38] Even so, if overseas capital markets offer higher expected yields, this may be reflected in lower premium rates and the premium outflow would be reduced. Currency matching can sometimes be forced on foreign reinsurers, particularly in respect of their proportional reinsurance treaties where regulatory laws may require ceding companies to hold on to premium balances; market competition may force reinsurers to accept that practice.

Balance-of-payments costs are often further reduced by commissions and other servicing costs paid to local residents.

Thus the overall balance-of-payments costs of insurance or reinsurance imports are substantially less than any superficial examination of the outflow of premium payments would suggest.

Establishment Business

The establishment of foreign companies locally results, generally, in lower direct balance-of-payments costs than the supply of insurance on a cross-frontier basis.

When a new branch or subsidiary is set up in a country the balance of payments of that country is usually strengthened by a capital inflow which will make a direct contribution to foreign-exchange reserves, even though part of the capital costs, in particular the capital deposit or solvency reserves, may be financed by a transfer of financial assets already held in the receiving country by the foreign parent organization. Sometimes, however, the entry of a foreign insurer to a country's insurance market may not make such a direct contribution to its balance of payments; for example, the foreign insurer may finance the acquisition of an existing local insurance company through an exchange of shares or through local borrowing.

Payments to the local personnel employed by the branch of the foreign insurance company, as well as corporate taxes paid to the government, reduce any surplus available for remittance to the parent company. Once established, it is common for foreign insurance companies to let the local organization grow at a pace dictated by the local generation of funds and to limit further external capital support. Thus a typical balance-of-payments profile for a newly-established organization is characterized by an initial capital inflow; then for a number of years, earnings will be ploughed back to finance growth and to satisfy local solvency requirements. Over time this favourable balance-of-payments picture for the host country will be reversed as profit remittances to the parent company are made. In the 1980s, however, because of the costs of financing an expanding volume of business, particularly in countries where inflation has been high, remittances have tended to be quite small in relation to the local equity stake.

An additional impact on the balance of payments may result from reinsurance outflows from the branch to the parent company, often as part of reinsurance agreements arranged on a global basis. If, however, the local market is large and conditions are conducive to establishment, the balance-of-payments cost may be reduced if reinsurers who have themselves established locally, arrange reinsurance, under the global arrangement, through their local organizations.

In its 1984 Report, *Insurance in the Context of Services and the Development Process*, the UNCTAD Secretariat contended that the head offices of foreign insurers influenced the reinsurance and investment decisions of their local branches and subsidiaries. This could be done by requiring more reinsurance to be directed into the company's worldwide agreements than would normally be the case, or by requiring the local branch or subsidiary to purchase foreign investments or to make external loans to other subsidiaries in the group. In respect of investment decisions, exchange-control regulations in most developing countries would preclude foreign investment but the other practices could adversely affect the balance-of-payments position of the host country. Because of its more liberal treatment by exchange-control authorities, reinsurance is sometimes the only way that a foreign insurer can secure a cash-flow return from its local branch or subsidiary if profit remittances and dividend payments are restricted. If such a policy is adopted, however, it is likely to be one of last resort.

Measures that are intended to discourage cross-frontier business, but permit establishment, will in most cases result in some balance-of-payments savings in the short run and probably in the long run too, although the extent will depend on local conditions. Savings on the balance of payments may be small. For example, if foreign companies which are prepared to establish are incapable of meeting domestic demand so that cross-frontier business still takes place. Indeed, if large multinational enterprises that are operating in the country are unable to obtain the insurances which they require from locally-based insurance companies, or if premium rates are considered to be excessively high, they may seek to obtain insurance cover through their parent organizations. The costs of these transactions could be defrayed through higher dividends or transfer pricing[39] so that the effect on the balance of payments of the host country may not be obvious.

The balance-of-payments repercussions of policies which also discourage the supply of insurance through the establishment of foreign insurance companies are even less clear. To the extent that local suppliers of insurance gain a larger market share, the balance-of-payments costs will be reduced, if the initial capital inflows associated with newly established foreign concerns are ignored. Such gains must be offset, however, against any increase in the amount of reinsurance which has to be purchased from abroad, perhaps at higher prices. By deterring large progressive international insurers from becoming established, a market loses the capacity and skill such companies can contribute towards maximizing the amount of business which can be retained locally, especially when their global-agreement reinsurance partners are also present in the market. Thus it may be argued that the establishment of large international insurers and reinsurers in a market can lead to a reduction in a country's overall balance-of-payments costs.

The extent to which the governments of many developing countries have been able to minimize the balance-of-payments costs of purchasing reinsurance from abroad by mobilizing internal capacity — for example, by the formation of state reinsurance corporations, or insisting on reciprocal reinsurance treaties, or through regional reinsurance pools — depends on a number of factors. Some are set out below.

(a) The benefits to be gained from an increase in local market retentions depends on the potential variability of claims costs[40] and, in particular, the foreign-exchange content of those costs. (In the case of insurances against natural disasters or other major catastrophes that occur infrequently, occurrence of the event may produce losses far exceeding any surplus built up over many years).

(b) Reciprocal reinsurance treaties may not necessarily prove profitable.

(c) The benefit to an individual country of participating in regional pools depends on the degree of cross-subsidization that occurs within the pool.[41]

Countries following such policies have invariably had to turn to international reinsurers for the additional capacity required for the larger risks. Because of the fragmentation of reinsurance markets caused by such practices, transaction costs and risk loadings in reinsurance market premiums increase which, in turn, reduce these balance-of-payments gains.

INDIRECT BALANCE-OF-PAYMENTS EFFECTS

We now look briefly at the indirect effects on the balance of payments of the supply of insurance by foreign companies.

First, labour and capital resources may be released by the removal of barriers to foreign suppliers of insurance because the foreign insurers take a share of the domestic market and local domestically-owned insurance companies go out of business. It is not difficult to envisage situations where freed resources of this kind might be deployed more efficiently elswhere in an economy and might produce exports worth more than the balance-of-payments costs associated with foreign supplies of insurance. For example, in a number of developing economies where the opportunity cost of capital is high, especially domestically-owned capital, any capital tied up in providing insurance services might be combined more usefully with surplus labour to assist the development of primary or manufacturing industries in which small to medium-size local firms may have a comparative advantage.[42] Moreover, an inward-looking market environment created by protective insurance legislation is not conducive to encouraging local insurers themselves to develop their own export potential.

Second, the overall adverse effects on the balance of payments of discouraging foreign supplies of insurance may more than outweigh any short-term saving on premium outflows. In this sense, it is important to remember the effect of barriers on the choice of insurance cover and the quality of service; how such factors may impair the ability of a local industry to compete against foreign firms or to attract investment by multinational enterprises; and how restrictions on transportation insurances may adversely affect international trade and thus the costs of a country's imports and exports. The UNCTAD Secretariat has stressed the necessity for developing countries to make greater efforts to increase 'the quality of insurance services provided to the local community'.[43]

GLOBAL ECONOMIC EFFECTS

Finally, it is worth mentioning briefly the global economic effects of these barriers to international insurance trade. There is much support for the view that the existence of barriers to trade on goods and services results in a sub-optimal allocation of resources and impairs the potential rate of economic growth.[44]

The diversion of economic resources to inefficient insurance companies forms a part of this more general issue. The greater degree of market fragmentation which arises from protective policies aimed at localizing premium balances has the effect of increasing the global amount of risk capital needed to cover global insurance needs. Moreover, uncertainty engendered by the existence of these market frictions has in the past periodically resulted in shortages of underwriting capacity for large-scale, technologically advanced innovations and this in turn is likely to have had a negative impact, albeit marginal, on economic growth. The level of world trade, too, is affected by policies which hinder the smooth running of markets for marine, aviation and other forms of transportation insurance.

NOTES AND REFERENCES

1. The example of the willingness of American insurers to offer the large 'deductibles' which major industrial companies demand is cited in R.K. Bishop, 'Recent and Future Developments in Underwriting: the International Scene', annual conference, Chartered Insurance Institute, London, 1976.

2. Ripoll, 'Some Thoughts on Development and Insurance', *op. cit.*

3. José Ripoll questions the lack of insurance against famine in India. His answer is that those who suffer could not afford the

premium. See Ripoll, *ibid.* In other words there is no effective demand to support commercial insurance. This wider question of the role of governments in subsidizing the purchase of fairly-priced commercial insurance, because of the economic welfare benefits conferred by insurance, is beyond the scope of this discussion. It is also worth noting here that private insurance markets cannot always supply insurance cover against catastrophic losses and they need to co-operate with governments. Flood insurance in the United States is a good example of this. See B. Berliner, *Limits of Insurability of Risks* (Englewood Cliffs, New Jersey: Prentice-Hall, 1982).

4. The maintenance of an adequate business network was listed by W.R. Malinowski as one of the guidelines foreign insurance companies operating in developing countries should observe. See Malinowski, *op. cit.*

5. A description of the difficulties raised by the imposition of restrictions on the insurance of imports and exports is contained in *Freedom of Transport Insurance* (Paris: International Chamber of Commerce, 1975). In encouraging developing countries to build up their own marine insurance markets, the UNCTAD study group recognized the problems and the need for international cooperation in the provision of claims handling facilities and so on. See *Marine Cargo Insurance*, *op. cit.*

6. The UNCTAD Secretariat has recognized that the domestic markets of many developing countries lack 'the professional specialization and ... level of insurance capacity' to underwrite big individual risks, *Insurance in the Context of Services and the Development Process*, Document TD/B/1014 (Geneva: UNCTAD Secretariat, 1984) p. 25.

7. Brian Hindley, *Economic Analysis and Insurance Policy in the Third World*, Thames Essay No. 32 (London: Trade Policy Research Centre, 1982) p. 20. Expenses and commissions account for a half of the premiums in many developing countries, which is far higher than in developed countries, although in 1982 operating costs as a percentage of non-life premiums in nine developed countries ranged from 24.4 per cent in Japan to 40.3 per cent in Spain. *Sigma*, Swiss Reinsurance Group, Zurich, February 1985.

8. Allegations that international insurers charge premium rates higher than the risk warrants in developing countries may possibly overlook this point. See Malinowski, *op. cit.*, and Ripoll, 'Some Thoughts on Development and Insurance', *op. cit.*

9. *Insurance in the Context of Services and the Development Process*, *op. cit.*, p. 18.

10. One of the explanations given by the UNCTAD Secretariat for the relatively high insurance costs in developing countries is that local insurers 'face the problem of a level of premium receipts too low to give a reasonable spread of risks, generally associated with insufficient diversity in the risks covered'. See *Loss Prevention in Fire and Marine Cargo Insurance*, Document TD/B/C3/162 (Geneva: UNCTAD Secretariat, 1980) p. 8.

11. For example, the influx of American companies into the international aviation market in the early 1970s resulted in airline premium rates being substantially reduced. Also see Note 2, Chapter 3, regarding Canadian premium rates.

12. Differences in both corporate tax rates and in tax rates on premiums can affect relative supply costs. Continental European insurers contend that the lower premiums which United Kingdom insurers charge for term life insurances are partly attributable to a more favourable United Kingdom system of taxation of life insurance companies. Finsinger, Hammond and Tapp, *op.cit.*, p. 131.

13. In J.S. Bain's terminology, existing insurers may tend to bring down premiums to the no-entry ceiling price; that is, a price sufficiently low to deter potential new entrants. See J.S. Bain, *Barriers to New Competition* (Cambridge, Massachusetts: Harvard University Press, 1956).

14. An analysis of the influence of premium rates on losses is contained in Doherty, *Insurance Pricing and Loss Prevention* (Farnborough, Hampshire: Saxon House, 1976) chs. 4-6. Mr. Doherty does, however, also stress the importance of consumer awareness of rating incentives.

15. The inadequacies of the premium rating practices of conventional insurers in both developed and developing countries, coupled with their unwillingness often to supply the types of insurance cover required by large industrial/commercial enterprises, have been a major factor influencing multinational and large domestic corporations to form their own captive insurance companies. This process has been aided by international reinsurers who have been more accommodating to the requirements of the captive insurers, so resulting in a substantial diversion of business from direct insurance to reinsurance markets. For an account of captive insurers, see *The Impact of Captive Insurance Companies on the Insurance Markets of Developing Countries*, Document TD/B/C3/192 (Geneva: UNCTAD Secretariat, 1984).

16. It is self-evident that adequate statistical data and expert interpretation thereof is a pre-condition of fairly discriminatory ratings systems. *Ibid.*

17. Although the competitive pressure admittedly came from new, mainly locally-owned companies, it was the rapid increase in the market share of independent companies which brought about the collapse of the motor insurance tariff in Britain in 1968. In the case of fire insurance, the loss of business to foreign (in particular American) companies has played a major role in the breakdown of the United Kingdom fire tariff since the late 1970s and its final abandonment in 1985.

18. See Carter, *Economics and Insurance* (Stockport, Cheshire: P.H. Press, 1972) p. 80; J.J. Rosa, 'Les economies des dimensions des institutions financieres', *Banque*, Paris, May 1972; Karl Borch, 'Administrative Expenses of Insurance Companies: an Experiment with Norwegian ‘Statistics', *Lettre d'Information*, Association Internationale pour l'Etude de l'Economie de l'Assurance, Geneva, October 1976; P. Praetz, 'A Note on Economies of Scale in the UK Property-liability Insurance Industry', *Journal of Risk and Insurance*, Athens, Georgia, June 1985.

19. An UNCTAD report on the localization of funds recognized that it should only extend to technical reserves. *Investment of the Technical Reserves of Insurance Concerns in the Country where the Premium Arises*, Document TD/B/C3/87 (Geneva: UNCTAD Secretariat, 1975).

20. A good analysis of the relationship between probability of ruin, levels of reserves, the cost of servicing reserves, reinsurance and the premium loading is provided in R.E. Beard, 'The Three R's of Insurance — Risk, Retention and Reinsurance', *Journal of the Institute of Actuaries Students Society*, Vol. 15, Pt 6, London, 1959, and in Carter, *Reinsurance*, 2nd edition (Brentford, Middlesex: Kluwer Publishing, 1983) ch. 9.

21. Malinowski, *op. cit.*, explained that some developing countries are placing great emphasis on state participation because of their lack of entrepreneurial talent. To exclude an external supply of a scarce resource hardly makes good economic sense and UNCTAD now not only recognizes that there is a shortage of adequately trained insurance personnel in many developing countries but that to allocate scarce resources to the insurance industry withdraws them from other, possibly more productive uses. *Insurance in the Context of Services and the Development Process*, *op. cit.*, p. 2.

22. The right of the British supervisory authority, for example, to ask overseas companies operating through branch offices in Britain to submit returns covering their worldwide business is the subject of regular criticism and has contributed to the decision of many to form United Kingdom registered subsidiary companies.

23. *Third World Insurance at the End of the 1970s*, Document TD/C/C3/169/Add.1/Rev.1 (Geneva: UNCTAD Secretariat, 1980) pp. 3-4. In 1984 UNCTAD once again reiterated that increased efforts should be made to remedy such deficiencies. See *Insurance in the Context of Services and the Development Process*, *op. cit.*

24. An outline of the educational and training needs of the industry can be found in the UNCTAD study report, *Insurance Education for Developing Countries*, Document TD/B/C3/121/Supp. 1 (Geneva: UNCTAD Secretariat, 1975).

25. The need for well-qualified staff for the successful undertaking of transportation insurances and reinsurance operations is recognized in the UNCTAD reports on *Marine Cargo Insurance*, *op. cit.*; *Reinsurance Problems in Developing Countries*, Document TD/B/C3/106 (Geneva: UNCTAD Secretariat, 1975), and *Insurance in the Context of Services and the Development Process*, *op. cit.*

26. This is the infant-industry argument for protection. See, for example, Bo Södersten, *International Economics* (London: Macmillan, 1970), p. 375.

27. For a good discussion of the problems of generalizing on this question, see Robert E. Baldwin, *Non-tariff Distortions to International Trade* (Washington: Brookings Institution, 1970).

28. Max Corden suggests that in developed economies the first-best solution is some form of wage subsidization. W.M. Corden, *Trade Policy and Economic Welfare* (Oxford: Oxford University Press, 1974) ch. 6. It has been suggested, however, that in developing countries the provision of employment is the only way in which income redistribution can be achieved. Paul Streeten and Frances Stewart, 'Conflict between Output and Employment Objectives in Developing Countries', in Streeten (ed.), *Frontiers of Development Studies* (London: Macmillan, 1972).

29. UNCTAD list the training of personnel in insurance and risk management amongst the potential positive contributions of foreign insurance companies to developing countries. *The Impact of Captive Insurance Companies*, *op. cit.*

30. See Raymond J. Krommenacker, *Les Nations Unies et l'Assurance Reassurance* (Paris: R. Pichon et R. Durand-Auzias, 1975).

For example, foreign life insurance companies operating in the Norwegian market presented keen competition for the emergent Norwegian companies in the mid-nineteenth century. See *Insurance Markets of the World* (Zurich: Swiss Reinsurance, 1964).

31. Hindley, *op. cit.*, p. 38.

32. Maurice Greenburg, President of the American International Group, based in New York, referring to the Managua and Guatemalan earthquake disasters, commented: 'To talk about self-sufficiency or domestication or nationalization of the insurance industry under these circumstances is nonsense. Neither is regionalization the answer. All of Central America could not have handled these losses'. 'International Problems and Possible Solutions', *op. cit.* J.A.S. Neave showed how the Mercantile and General Reinsurance Company had helped to spread the Flixborough (United Kingdom) and Darwin (Australia) disasters over 46 and 51 countries respectively. Neave, 'The Effect on International Reinsurance of Changing Patterns in Economic Relationships', *op. cit.* UNCTAD also recognizes the dangers: see the report *Investment of the Technical Reserves of Insurance Concerns*, *op. cit.*, p. 7.

33. It is arguable that the mere existence of institutions such as life offices encourages a larger volume of personal saving than otherwise would occur and life insurers do not play a merely passive role — they go out and seek savings. See Carter, *Economics and Insurance*, *op. cit.*, p. 37; and P.C.I. Ayre, 'The Future of Private Foreign Investment in Less Developed Countries', in T.J. Byrne (ed.), *Foreign Resources and Economic Development* (London: Frank Cass, 1972) p. 13.

34. See Hindley, *op. cit.*, pp. 28-33.

35. See Milton Friedman, 'The Case for Flexible Exchange Rates', in Caves and Harry G. Johnson (eds), *Readings in International Economics* (Homewood Illinois: Richard D. Irwin, for the American Economic Association, 1968); and Robert M. Stern, *The Balance of Payments* (London: Macmillan, 1974).

36. For a fuller discussion, see Dickinson, *International Insurance Transactions and the Balance of Payments*, *op. cit.*

37. See H. Louberge, *Reinsurance and the Foreign Exchange Risk*, Geneva Papers on Risk and Insurance No. 11 (Geneva: Association Internationale pour l'Etude de l'Economie de l'Assurance, 1979) and C. Worthington, 'Exchange Rate Risks and their Impact on Reinsurance Companies', paper presented to the Second Meeting

of Insurance Economists, University of Nottingham, 1980.

38. Since in countries where local capital markets are rudimentary local enterprises often have difficulty raising finance for expansion, insurance companies not infrequently make finance available, usually in the form of loans, as a means of strengthening their commercial links in the expectation that they will gain more insurance business from these enterprises as they grow.

39. In discussing the use by multinationals of captive insurance companies, the UNCTAD Secretariat has observed: 'A captive may reinsure a (local) fronting company for locally available coverages, and issue direct insurance in the form of a difference in conditions policy to provide coverages not available in the local market' (para 62). With regard to premium rating it concluded that 'The ultimate effect of such excessively high rates can be detrimental to the host country. Less insurance is ultimately purchased since companies can often find ways to bypass these high rates. Moreover, less money might be invested in the local economy if insurance is bought outside' (para 128). See *The Impact of Captive Insurance Companies*, *op. cit.*

40. See Ripoll, 'Some Thoughts on Development and Insurance', *op. cit.*

41. For a discussion of reciprocal reinsurance arrangements and pools in general, see the UNCTAD study, *Reinsurance Problems in Developing Countries, op. cit.* An examination of the performance of the Arab regional reinsurance arrangements can be found in A.Z.A. Ali, *Insurance Development in the Arab World* (London: Graham & Trotman, 1985).

42. UNCTAD has recognized the possible existence of such costs. See *Insurance in the Context of Services and the Development Process, op. cit.*, para. 41.

43. It adds that 'Terms, prices and conditions of local insurance are expected to have a positive influence on the whole production and distribution process, including export promotion'. *Ibid*, p. 4.

44. See John R. Hicks, *Essays in World Economics* (Oxford: Oxford University Press, 1957); and Johnson, *Comparative Costs and Commercial Policy Theory for a Developing World Economy* (Stockholm: Almqvist & Wicksell, 1968).

Chapter 6

Towards Greater Freedom of Trade in Insurance

THE PRECEDING four chapters have explained why governments have restricted trade in insurance, the nature of those restrictions and the economic consequences thereof. This chapter summarizes the argument for trade liberalization in insurance services. In the following chapter we examine the progress which the member states of the European Community have been able to make towards their aim of removing all restrictions on trade in insurance and reinsurance in the Community in order to see what lessons the European experience may hold for global trade negotiations. The concluding chapter will consider the discussions that have already taken place and those that are currently under way within the wider international fora of the OECD and the GATT, covering the liberalization of the insurance trade. Finally, we make some suggestions for facilitating progress in those discussions.

It is possible for all countries to benefit from the pursuit of policies aimed at the relaxation of restrictions on trade in insurance, including those that will import more insurance/ reinsurance cover than they do under a restrictive regime. This study has stressed the significant economic cost that can arise within an economy that does not possess adequate risk transfer facilities. An analogy can be drawn between the role of insurance as a risk transfer facility in an economy and the role of a lubricant in the running of an engine. The lubricant can only be judged on how it contributes to the efficient running of the engine.

FREEDOM OF CHOICE IN INSURANCE
AND REINSURANCE

In the competitive markets in which international insurance and reinsurance companies operate, consumers would, in general, gain more if foreign insurers were free to choose between supplying insurance and reinsurance on a cross-frontier or on an establishment basis rather than having the choice imposed on them by governments. Generally, insurers offering direct insurance tend to differ from those offering reinsurance on the conditions necessary to supply a competitive service. In most markets, those offering direct insurance will have difficulty in competing unless they have a local establishment to provide an on-the-spot service to local consumers. This incentive to establish a presence is quite independent of any legislative, fiscal and relative resource-cost considerations. Therefore, unless it is felt that the volume of business would not warrant the costs involved, an insurance company offering direct insurance would in most cases prefer, political risk factors apart, to operate as an established insurer in any country which is an important source of business.

Lloyd's of London, for the most part, supplies insurance on a cross-frontier basis and so do the other insurance exchanges that have been formed over the last decade. Lloyd's and the insurance exchanges do have the advantage, however, that the major insurance brokers that bring business to them make available their own overseas networks of offices to provide the necessary pre-sales and post-sales servicing of business. Yet in spite of these service supports it is not coincidental that over a half of the property and liability insurance placed across frontiers with Lloyd's in London now comes in the form of reinsurance rather than direct insurance.

Reinsurers are in a somewhat different position. Establishment can provide some advantages, which have induced the major reinsurance companies to establish offices and/or subsidiary companies in all of the world's major insurance and reinsurance centres. But establishment is not so important for reinsurance companies as it is for companies offering direct insurance, especially in view of the growth of information technology. More fundamental to the growth of international reinsurance is:

(a) the freedom of companies offering direct insurance to determine their own reinsurance needs and to select their reinsurance contracts and reinsurers accordingly; and

(b) for reinsurers to be able to control the investment of their funds and to be free from exchange-control restrictions so that they can pay promptly their claim obligations anywhere in the world.

RESTRICTIONS ON CROSS-FRONTIER INSURANCE

It has been shown that some countries prohibit or discourage cross-frontier insurance of all kinds for overt political reasons. If a government knowingly prefers to subordinate economic efficiency to political ideology that is its concern. Restrictions on cross-frontier insurance business are often allegedly based on economic criteria, but we doubt whether governments carry out a comprehensive economic cost/benefit analysis of the effects of discouraging or prohibiting foreign sources of insurance supply.[1] Often legislation is instituted as a part of a wider commercial policy aimed at greater import substitution. One economic reason for restricting cross-frontier insurance arises from balance-of-payments considerations. Such restrictions, as a rule, have been part of exchange-control policies imposed on outward payment and capital flows. In Chapter 5, it was shown that the balance-of-payments benefits arising from discouraging insurance trade are likely to be comparatively small and when wider economic factors are taken into account the overall impact on the balance of payments may even be in the opposite direction. If a government, however, feels constrained to have some form of exchange control, it should pay particular attention to the wider effects arising from restrictions on insurance trade and be prepared to consider a more selective treatment than at present.

Governments, of course, have a responsibility to ensure that individual policyholders are protected against dishonest and incompetent management, especially with regard to long-term insurance. But such arguments are less persuasive when applied to corporate buyers of insurance, since the risk associated with the choice of insurance contract or insurance supplier is a commercial risk. The same could be said of reinsurance where both of the contracting parties are insurance professionals. There is concern among some governments, however, that the failure of a reinsurer could have a domino effect which would undermine the solvency of the local companies and thus eventually the security of local policyholders. But supervisory authorities in countries which import insurance should seek to rely more on their counterparts in the exporting countries. It is worth observing that an implicit transfer of supervisory responsibility (to the supervisory authorities in the countries where foreign reinsurers are located) already exists in a large number of cases in respect of cross-frontier insurance. It has also been suggested that an international register of reinsurers based on common codes and requirements should be established.[2]

Obstacles to cross-frontier transactions often arise because of government policies aimed at protecting a local insurance industry. It is doubtful, however, whether the creation of a protected local market is always the best environment for the development by local insurers of their export potential.

As far as personal insurances are concerned, the majority of consumers prefer to arrange cover with locally-based companies. Restrictions on the foreign supply of cross-frontier life insurance would be unlikely to impair consumer welfare significantly at present, but, with rapid improvements in communications technology and increasing consumer awareness, this is likely to change. In the provision of corporate insurance the situation is different. Corporate buyers are much less parochial. They base their decisions to buy insurance on price and quality of service.

Attempts to liberalize direct insurance supplied on a cross-frontier basis within the European Community have proved difficult, even though a prior commitment exists to create a free market in insurance. This would suggest that attempts to develop a more liberal environment for international direct insurance will be far from easy. The position for reinsurance is perhaps somewhat more hopeful in that reinsurance business currently is much less regulated by governments, although not all signs portend well in this direction.[3]

INSURANCE SUPPLIED THROUGH LOCAL ESTABLISHMENTS

In the main, although insurance supplied directly by foreign insurers through local establishment does not conflict with national political, economic or fiduciary concerns to the same degree as insurance supplied on a cross-frontier basis, it is, nevertheless, in many developed and developing countries subject to restrictions. Furthermore, establishment through incorporation as a local subsidiary conflicts less with the national objectives of some countries than establishment through a local branch or agency. Governments often over-estimate the conflict with national economic interests and the potential threat to policyholder security, although they usually exist to some degree. It is likely to be a difficult process to persuade governments or regulatory authorities that the gains from liberalization of the insurance trade may be more important than potential short-term difficulties.

It is rare for governments to have realistic perceptions of the role of foreign insurance enterprises in the local economy (even when they operate through local subsidiaries). For example, multinational enterprises in manufacturing and extractive industries are more capital-intensive and employ more technologically-advanced production methods than insurance companies and the benefits to host countries are more apparent. Moreover, these manufacturing multinationals exercise less control over the flow of funds to local capital markets and have a more limited scope to transfer funds abroad than insurance companies. Therefore, where the climate of opinion has been unfavourable to multinational enterprises in general, multinational insurance enterprises have usually been exposed to even more adverse criticism. It has been argued that much of the criticism has been misplaced and that the benefits to be derived from allowing freedom of establishment for foreign insurance companies, both to the economy in general and to domestic policyholders in particular, have often been under-estimated.

It would seem, therefore, that the interests of virtually all countries would be best served by allowing freedom of establishment, although the desire of governments to protect domestic policyholders and to exercise control over the movement and investment of funds must be respected. Thus, foreign insurance companies must expect to be subject to the same rules as locally-owned companies, although in some cases it would be in everyone's interest for some of the rules to be relaxed.

Non-discrimination would imply that all countries should permit the entry of foreign insurance companies to their domestic insurance markets on the same conditions as those applying to locally-owned companies. This proposal is in accord with the guidelines for national treatment contained in the declaration on International Investment and Multinational Enterprises adopted by the member governments of the OECD in June 1976.[4] In turn, the companies should adhere to the guidelines for behaviour set out in the same declaration. Of particular importance to insurance companies are the following guidelines which propose that they should:

(a) take fully into account established policy objectives of the member countries in which they operate (which would mean in the case of an insurance company such matters as economic development and the creation of employment opportunities);

(b) in managing the financial and commercial operations of their activities, and especially their liquid foreign assets and liabilities, take into account the established objectives of the countries in which they operate regarding balance-of-payments and credit policies; and

(c) refrain from making use of the particular facilities available to them, such as transfer pricing which does not conform to an arm's length standard, for modifying in ways contrary to national laws the tax base on which members of the group are assessed. The particular facility available to insurers is, of course, reinsurance arranged with a parent company or another subsidiary in the group.

It would be naïve, however, to believe that acceptance of the guidelines by the governments of host and investing countries and the companies themselves will resolve all of the problems and conflicts, as negotiations within the European Community have amply shown. Consistency in insurance supervisory regulations will ensure that the policies of individual governments in the field of consumer protection *et cetera* can still operate without distorting competition between locally-owned and foreign-owned companies established in each national market.

In the rest of this chapter, some specific proposals will be put forward to deal with some of the issues raised regarding the freedom of establishment and the removal of the discriminatory measures which exist throughout the world.

LOCAL REGISTRATION, SHAREHOLDERS AND MANAGEMENT

If it is likely that the unsatisfied claims of policyholders in one country cannot be enforced easily against an insurance company which has its head office or holds its funds in another country, a case can be made for requiring any foreign company that wishes to establish a local organization to form a locally-incorporated subsidiary. The case is not strong and it has been pointed out earlier that there are costs associated with the geographical fragmentation of capital funds. Some governments maintain, however, that even if it means that domestic consumers must pay more for their insurances it is a reasonable price to pay for ensuring greater control and improved security. There is a need, however, for an international system which will ensure security for the policyholder but will permit companies to establish through a local branch or agency, rather than having to incorporate as a local subsidiary with the attendant higher costs.

Although governments may like to see the control of institutions such as insurance companies in local hands, the case for enforcing local shareholdings is even less persuasive. Local ownership is neither a necessary nor a sufficient condition to ensure that companies behave in accordance with the public interest.[5] Governments should realize that forcing foreign insurance companies to share the ownership of their subsidiaries with local interests, especially if this results in a minority shareholding position for the foreign company, will tend to discourage further investment by companies and could cause them to leave the market. This can apply even if the foreign company retains management control because the longer term prospects would be less certain.

Likewise, the imposition of excessive restrictions on the issue of work permits for expatriate personnel operates against the national interest, for reasons already discussed in an earlier chapter. While the OECD guidelines for employment and industrial relations go a long way, compulsion can be counter-productive.

DIFFERENTIAL CAPITAL AND SOLVENCY REGULATIONS

If a foreign insurance company chooses to establish a locally-incorporated subsidiary there is no case for subjecting it to more stringent capital and/or solvency regulations than those which apply to locally-owned companies.

If a company is allowed to trade by establishing a local branch, a government may wish to ensure that adequate assets are maintained locally to cover expected liabilities to policyholders, calculated to include possible fluctuations in claims costs and other contingencies.[6] Furthermore, as an additional safeguard, it is understandable that all or part of such assets should be deposited locally. In this case the costs of fragmenting capital funds may be a price that has to be paid. There is no reason, however, for requiring foreign companies to maintain capital funds locally that are either (i) disproportionately larger than those required of locally-incorporated companies or (ii) invested in a more restricted range of securities, possibly government securities, than those from which locally-incorporated companies are allowed to choose. Either type of measure places foreign companies at a disadvantage and distorts competition.

REINSURANCE REGULATIONS

Some element of control over reinsurance arrangements is a normal part of the supervision of insurance companies. Moreover, it is not surprising that countries experiencing balance-of-payments difficulties seek to prevent outflows of reinsurance premiums by forming state reinsurance corporations, imposing compulsory cessions and so on. We have pointed out the potential net costs such policies entail, but if a government nevertheless still proceeds with such measures, there can be no justification for subjecting foreign-owned companies to more stringent treatment than domestic insurers regarding either the size of compulsory cessions or the reinsurance rates allowed thereon.

Also, although the ceding of business to overseas parent companies may be used sometimes as a means of minimizing local tax payments or as a form of transfer pricing, less harmful ways are available to control such practices than a universal ban on placing reinsurances abroad.

NOTES AND REFERENCES

1. Harold Skipper questions whether governments always do act rationally. Even when they do they may not accept that liberalization

is economically desirable. It is what Dr. Skipper calls a '*status quo*' factor at work. See Skipper, 'Protectionism in Provision of International Insurance Services', *op. cit.*

2. B. Densmore, 'World Register of Reinsurers Should be Established', *Business Insurance*, Chicago, 10 May 1982.

3. For example, New York State, followed by some other American states, has introduced more stringent regulations governing non-admitted reinsurance and the UNCTAD Secretariat, while it has to some degree modified its position regarding the formation of domestic reinsurance corporations, continues to press for regional co-operation in insurance and reinsurance and recommends that 'foreign reinsurance should be acquired to make up only for shortages of local insurance capacity'. See *Insurance in the Context of Services and the Development Process*, *op. cit.*, p. 4.

4. *International Investment and Multinational Enterprises* (Paris: OECD Secretariat, 1976).

5. Local managements are not infrequently accused of failing to act in the public interest. For example, see the criticism of the investment behaviour of banks and insurance companies in Britain contained in the policy statement on banking and finance prepared by the Labour Party's National Executive Committee (1976). A government can always exercise control without taking over the ownership of a company. See Carter, 'Further Comment on Insurance and Development', *Best's Review*, April 1976.

6. The European Community's directives on Freedom of Establishment for Life and Non-life Insurance, for example, includes such provisions for insurance companies not incorporated in a member country of the Community.

Chapter 7

European Community's Efforts to Liberalize Insurance Trade

AS PART of the wider aims under Article 3 of the Treaty of Rome, which was signed in 1957, there was the specific aim of creating a common market in insurance. According to the original timetable, it was to have been achieved by 1969. Such a market would permit insurers with head offices in any part of the European Community:

(a) to establish branches (or subsidiaries) in any other country within the Community ('freedom of establishment'); and

(b) to sell insurance across national frontiers within the Community ('freedom of services').[1]

Today freedom of establishment is a reality for both insurers and intermediaries within the European Community and there has been some movement towards the integration of national markets within the rest of Western Europe. More than twenty years after the 1969 deadline, however, cross-frontier business for direct insurance still has not been fully implemented.

A detailed summary of the progress that has been made towards the removal of the legal obstacles to the creation of a common insurance market in the European Community is contained in Appendix III. This chapter will concentrate principally on examining the difficulties that have had to be overcome to enable insurers in the Community to open establishments anywhere within the Community and on the reasons for the Community's failure so far to achieve complete liberalization of insurance trade after almost 30 years of continuous negotiations.

OBSTACLES TO LIBERALIZATION

Although there was agreement in principle that insurance trade should be conducted freely between the states forming the European Community, it soon became clear that there were formidable obstacles to be overcome before it could become an operational reality for direct insurance. The position was markedly different for reinsurance in that reinsurance transactions within the Community were already relatively free, even between countries with tight regulation of direct insurance and/or extensive exchange controls. Therefore, it was agreed to seek, in the first instance, freedom for reinsurance both on an 'establishment' and a 'services' basis. A reinsurance directive that embraced both freedoms was produced comparatively quickly in 1964.

In the case of direct insurance, one of the major obstacles to trade liberalization was the widely differing views of member governments on the means of protecting consumers of insurance. Since the end of the 19th century, the British Government has been content to pursue a policy of 'freedom with publicity', regulating the financial solvency of insurance companies while relying on market competition to produce the variety of insurance services required at adequate but not excessive prices. Market entry was relatively easy; new insurance companies had to have only a comparatively low level of paid-up capital and a prescribed excess of assets over liabilities. Once established, companies retained considerable freedom as to the manner in which they conducted their insurance business, including their pricing, marketing and investment decisions. They were obliged to continue to meet only the minimum solvency requirement and to make annual accounting returns to the then Board of Trade. The failure of a number of new companies in the early 1960s, however, revealed the need for the supervisory authority (now the Department of Trade and Industry) to be able to exercise more control over new entrants and to have wider powers of intervention. Therefore, after 1967, more stringent regulations were progressively introduced controlling both entry to the market and the conduct of business. These regulations imposed little extra constraint, however, on the manner in which well-established and financially prudent companies managed their affairs. Lloyd's underwriting syndicates were entirely free from official control, the Lloyd's market operating under a system of self-regulation administered by the Committee and the Council of Lloyd's.

Continental insurers, on the other hand, generally enjoyed far less commercial freedom. The supervisory authorities in France, the Federal Republic of Germany and Italy in particular not only exercised more stringent control over entry to, and exit from, their insurance markets and over the financial condition of companies but also regulated premium rates, policy coverage and contract terms, the marketing of insurance and the investment of insurance funds. There was a presumption in the Federal Repulic of Germany, for example, that the interests of consumers are best protected by ensuring that insurance companies supply standard services at prices that minimize the risk of insurers being unable to fulfil their commitments to policyholders. Such a paternalistic view of consumer protection extends in France and Italy to preventing residents from placing their insurances abroad with foreign insurers over whom the French or Italian supervisory authority can exercise no control. Although Germans are not precluded from arranging such cross-frontier insurances, German brokers are prohibited from helping them to do so.

Given such basic philosophical differences, it is not surprising that member countries continue to disagree on certain issues. For example, it has not been possible to reach agreement on a directive on insurance contract law to lay down coordinated rules applicable to all member countries regarding such matters as the information to be contained in policies, changes in risk during the term of the contract and the conditions dealing with the cancellation of policies. Therefore, the Life and Non-life

'Services' Directives limit the choice of law for policies, though the draft Non-life 'Framework' Directive will give corporate buyers, who need less protection, greater freedom for 'large risks'.

The obstacles to agreement extend also to the differing self-interests of insurance companies as they perceive them. Regulation of competition can protect not only consumers but also the providers of insurance services. Moreover, the British insurance industry, with its extensive overseas business, was determined that the European Community should not adopt regulations that would unfairly discriminate against third-country insurers. The adoption of a liberal trading policy *vis-à-vis* the outside world would, however, expose insurers in some member countries to new competition from third-country insurers as well as from other Community insurers.

Finally, there were differences bearing on competitive conditions regarding such matters as insurance contract law, the enforcement of contracts and taxation of insurance consumers and insurance companies. Therefore, it was recognized from the outset that 'establishment' would have to be the first step, with 'cross-frontier' insurance following later. Indeed, the introduction of 'freedom of services' for life and non-life insurance was made conditional on the prior introduction of 'freedom of establishment', the coordination of insurance contract law and the simplication of procedures to provide for the reciprocal enforcement of judgments.[2]

FREEDOM OF ESTABLISHMENT

Initially it was argued that 'freedom of establishment' should be conditional on the approximation of all laws 'to the extent necessary for the proper functioning of the common market'. This embraced laws affecting the competitive positions of insurers established in different member countries. Eventually, acceptable compromises were agreed and a directive intro-ducing 'freedom of establishment' for non-life insurance was adopted in 1973 and became effective in 1976, although some member countries did not finally amend their laws until ten years later.

Before agreement could be reached on the terms of a directive for life insurance, the Court of Justice of the European Community decided in 1974, in the case of *Reyners* v. *Belgian State*, that an automatic right of establishment had existed since 1970. Therefore, the directive adopted in 1979 'facilitated' rather than 'introduced' freedom of establishment for life insurance. It came into force, for the most part, in 1981.

The somewhat protracted discussions leading to the granting of freedom for insurers in the European Community to set up branch offices and subsidiaries in other member countries centred around the absolute right of access provided under the Treaty of Rome on terms equivalent to those applicable to locally-incorporated insurers. Eventually it was accepted that a uniform system of regulation throughout the Community was not necessary in order to ensure adequate policyholder protection and fair competition. Instead both the non-life and life directives focussed on:

(a) coordinating the conditions that an insurer must fulfil in order to obtain authorization to transact insurance business from an establishment in a member country;

(b) setting minimum standards of solvency for non-life and life insurance which the supervisory authority of the member country in which an insurer has its head office is responsible for supervising; and

(c) requiring an insurer to maintain in each member country in which it operates assets equal to its technical liabilities in that country, although individual member countries are free to administer their own rules regarding types of eligible assets and the valuation of assets and liabilities.

The life insurance directive also provides for the separation of the management of life and non-life business so as to safeguard the separate interests of life and non-life policyholders. It prohibited new composite companies but that restriction will be lifted following the 1991 review of existing composites.

Apart from the above, each member country in the European Community is free to decide whether to regulate other aspects of the operations of all insurers established in its country, including the branch offices of insurers established in other member countries, in respect of business written there. The result is that all insurers established in a member country do so on the same competitive footing; they have to adhere to local regulations, irrespective of the degree of stringency of those regulations. It is also worth observing that the supervisory authorities have not, apart from initial adjustment problems, been unduly dilatory in granting licences to Community insurers wishing to gain access to a national market.

INSURANCE INTERMEDIARIES DIRECTIVE

Further progress towards the creation of a common Community insurance market in the European Community was made in 1976 with the adoption of the Insurance Intermediaries Directive. This introduced transitional measures to facilitate, as from 1978, the exercise of the 'freedoms of establishment' and 'freedom of services' for Community insurance brokers and agents. Persons wishing to take advantage of the freedoms must comply with certain requirements set out in the directive and, until the 'freedom of services' for insurances becomes operative, they are not allowed to arrange cross-frontier insurances contrary to national laws. Subject to those conditions, however, national regulations requiring professional or other qualifications no longer bar Community agents or brokers resident in one part of the Community from operating in other member countries.[3]

Thus substantial progress has been made towards the ultimate objective of dismantling within the European Community all the legal barriers to insurance trade, leaving only 'freedom of services' for direct insurance still to be achieved.

'FREEDOM OF SERVICES' FOR DIRECT INSURANCE

It had been expected at the outset that the implementation of a 'services' directive for life insurance would not be feasible until there was freedom of capital movements within the European Community. Many other obstacles arising out of supervisory regulations relating to premium rating, policy coverage and permitted investments, and the tax treatment of life insurance premiums, policy benefits and life insurance companies would also have to be resolved. In 1985, the Commission declared in its White Paper entitled *Completing the Internal Market*, that a directive should be adopted for life insurance by 1992 and it commissioned a study of the obstacles that would have to be overcome. The study confirmed that even an attempt to make progress by limiting 'freedom of services' in the first instance to term-life insurances, which basically contain no savings element, would be fraught with difficulties.[4] But the need for individuals to be able to purchase life insurances and pensions contracts, denominated in currencies of their choice, across national frontiers, is becoming increasingly more important with the growth in the movement of labour between member countries.

The delay in making progress with regard to non-life insurance was less predictable. Following the decision of the European Court of Justice in 1974 in the *Van Binsbergen* case that 'freedom of services' for insurance already existed and that any directives on 'services' would in effect be facilitating the operation of this freedom, a draft 'services' directive for non-life insurance was prepared and published by the Commission in 1975. The extent to which the existing laws of member countries constituted a restriction on 'freedom of service' remained uncertain and so member countries could not reach agreement on a variety of technical issues relating to policyholder protection. Clearly the unwelcome prospect for some member countries of enhanced competition in local markets also lay behind the failure to agree on a directive. Several revised drafts of the non-life 'services' directive were subsequently prepared, but agreement still could not be reached on a number of issues.

An attempt to make some progress towards full 'freedom of services' for non-life insurance occurred in 1978 with the adoption of the Co-insurance Directive which was designed to facilitate the supply of non-life insurance across internal frontiers in the European Community for large industrial, commercial and transport risks. As argued earlier, such facilities are more important for the insurance of large risks than for personal and smaller business risks, given the current state of communications technology. Moreover, the fiduciary concern with regard to corporate insurance purchases is somewhat less than for personal insurances. Therefore, the directive, which came into force in 1980, provided for insurers in any member country to participate in the insurance of risks 'which by reason of their nature or size call for the participation of several insurers for their coverage'. Member countries in implementing the Co-insurance Directive, however, interpreted it in different ways. Two particular areas of disagreement arose. One related to the interpretation of 'nature or size' of risk in that some governments specified that co-insurance can only operate for risks of a size exceeding large monetary thresholds. The other concerned the interpretation of the directive by France, Denmark, Ireland and the Federal Republic of Germany as permitting them to require that the leading insurer in any co-insurance arrangement should have an establishment in the country where the risk is located; this interpretation was disputed by the Netherlands and the United Kingdom. The key role in arranging the insurances for large risks is played by the leading insurer who normally decides the premium, cover and policy terms which the co-insurers agree to follow.

Not surprisingly, given such differing interpretations of the directive and the resulting confusion, its implementation had little impact on the amount of cross-frontier co-insurance business actually transacted. In part this could be explained by the fact that, although technically different, reinsurance provides an alternative to co-insurance for spreading risks associated with large potential losses, so that even with greater freedom in cross-frontier co-insurance the flow of co-insurance is unlikely to be large, since the reinsurance networks are well developed. Nevertheless, if large buyers of insurance could choose insurers able to provide the most suitable contracts, it probably would create some additional demand for cross-frontier co-insurance.

From a trade point of view, therefore, the key question is the degree of freedom which is granted to buyers of insurance to choose their leading insurers from anywhere within the European Community. In 1985, the Commission decided to put the issue to the test by taking the Federal Republic of Germany, Denmark, France and Ireland to the European Court of Justice (Cases 205/84, 252/83, 220/83, and 206/84). The Court held in its judgment, delivered in December 1986, that, as contended by the Commission, the leading insurer need not have an establishment in the country of risk. It accepted, however, as a criterion for defining 'size' the monetary thresholds introduced by individual member countries.

The case against the Federal Republic of Germany also included a second issue which arose out of the action of the Federal Republic's supervisory authority in prosecuting a German broker. The broker was prosecuted for contravening the national insurance laws by placing direct insurance for German clients with insurance companies in London that were not established and authorized to write the business in the Federal Republic. The German broker appealed to the European Commission. The Court held that the German Government, by restricting German intermediaries to dealing with locally established insurers, had failed to fulfil its treaty obligations in the European Community in relation to the freedom to provide insurance services.

On the general issue of 'freedom of services', the Court held that while an insurer in the European Community should be able to provide insurance services to the residents of member countries in which it is not established:

(a) countries were justified in operating an authorization procedure for companies wishing to supply cross-frontier insurances and that generally, in order to protect policyholders, authorization could require compliance with the host country's mandatory rules regarding the calculation and localization of technical reserves, their investment in locally approved assets and possibly policy coverage and conditions; and

(b) if an insurer wishes to maintain a 'permanent presence' in, or direct its business entirely or principally towards the host country, it must be established.

The Court did not rule on the following three other matters related to the provision of cross-frontier insurance:

(a) the supply of compulsory insurances;

(b) transport insurances; and

(c) insurances where the policyholder and the risk are located in different countries.

Although the Court's decisions did not go as far as the Commission had hoped, they did provide some guidance regarding the principles on which further negotiations for implementing freedom of services for non-life insurance could be based. A further possible obstacle was removed by another decision of the European Court of Justice, given in January 1987, that the recommendations by the German Property Insurance Association to its members regarding premiums for fire and consequential loss insurances were contrary to the European Community's anti-competition rules and affected trade between member countries. A breakthrough came in a ministerial agreement in December 1987 to proceed with a second directive to free cross-frontier trade in non-life insurance which was finally approved in June 1988. The directive distinguishes between 'large risks' and 'mass risks'. Regarding the former, the intention is that after a phasing-in stage lasting until 31 December 1992 (with further extensions until January 1997 for Spain and January 1999 for Greece, Ireland and Portugal), Community companies will be free to purchase their insurances from insurers established anywhere in the Community; there will be no restrictions applying to transport, credit and suretyship, risks but for all other risks, the company must qualify as 'large' by meeting two out of three size criteria (see Appendix III). The directive supplements the 1973 Establishment Directive by introducing flexible rules for the currency matching of assets and liabilities which will apply to both establishment and cross-frontier business. Insurances supplied across frontiers will also be subject to the tax provisions of the purchaser's country. The proposed Insurance Accounts directive provides for the harmonization of technical reserves.

Although technically the Directive also provides for the freeing of trade in 'mass risks' (that is, personal and small commercial insurances), in practice, however, insurers wishing to transact such business will be subject to so many restrictions that little business is likely to be done. Before cross-frontier trade in 'mass risks' can become a reality, agreement will have to be reached on a variety of measures contained in the proposed 'Framework' Directives that will affect the solvency of insurers and the interests of consumers.

The Commission took the view that the Court's decision also made possible some progress with regard to life insurance for individuals who are willing to waive their rights to the protection afforded by the laws of the country in which they are resident. Consequently the Life Insurance Services Directive which was adopted in 1990 and is due to come into force in 1993, covers most types of life insurance other than contracted out pensions, but limits freedom to buy life insurances across borders to individuals (or firms) who, on their own initiative seek out an insurer in another member state. Although individuals eventually will be able to seek the help of a local intermediary, it leaves untouched the vast majority of personal insurances and group pension schemes to be dealt with by further directives.

Instead of progressing on a piecemeal basis, the Commission is now seeking to complete the single market for insurances services by means of two 'framework' directives covering non-life and life insurances respectively. The two draft directives are based on the same single licence or 'passport' principle as that already employed for banking and other financial services, i.e. coordination of the essential supervisory rules on prudential supervision; the mutual recognition by member states of a single authorization of an insurer issued by the member state in which its head office is located (its 'home country'); and the supervision of an insurer's entire business by its 'home' supervisory authority. If the directives are adopted without major revisions, a Community insurer will eventually be able to sell its services anywhere within the EC, either from establishments or across borders, subject only to 'home country' control, other than for compliance with non-discriminatory rules issued by the host country 'in the public good'. Subsidiaries, being local insurance companies, will be subject to host country control. Both directives also require the abandonment of regulations requiring systematic notification or prior approval of contract documents and premium rates.

TRADE WITH THIRD-COUNTRY INSURERS

In its relations with the rest of the world, the European Community seeks, in principle, to provide insurers from non-Community countries with access to its insurance markets. Third-country insurers, however, will be at a disadvantage if they operate through local branches rather than setting up a locally-incorporated subsidiary company. In particular, local branch companies have to fulfil more stringent financial conditions in respect of local asset holdings. Not all Community countries allow easy access to their local insurance markets. Where access is made difficult it is because the established insurance companies fear the competition which some of the major foreign insurance companies could present.

A weakness of the discussions on liberalization within the European Community has been an undue focus on legal and supervisory aspects. Insufficient attention has been paid to the economic and financial issues such as: the costs associated with the fragmentation of central capital; the costs associated with the use of conservative and inflexible bases for valuing assets and liabilities for solvency purposes; and the continued use of 'gross reserving' practices in reinsurance.

Regarding relationships with third country insurers, the Establishment directives enabled foreign insurers to gain access to the whole Commuity by setting up in one member state a locally incorporated subsidiary which would then qualify as a Community insurer. Following objections from Japan and the USA to the originally proposed provisions in the Life Insurance Services Directive for 'mirror image' trade reciprocity for future access to Community markets, the requirements were changed to a 'national treatment' basis, with a grandfathering provision for third country insurers already established within the EC. That brought the EC position on trade in financial services into line with both the US position and the GATT requirement of 'national treatment' for trade in goods.

Agreement between the European Community and Switzerland

In mid-1989 agreement was finalized between the Community and Switzerland giving insurers reciprocal access to each other's markets, subject to the same terms as apply within the Community.

Even though the agreement is only concerned with non-life establishment business and has yet to be implemented, it does raise a useful precedent for extending the intra-Community agreements on insurance trade to embrace other countries. In the case of Switzerland, agreement on establishment has been facilitated by the fact that the country's supervisory legislation and procedures already meet the minimum criteria which are specified within the European Community's Non-life Establishment Directive. The success of the agreement would demonstrate that access to national markets through establishment is possible so long as acceptable supervisory arrangements are made.

NOTES AND REFERENCES

1. Instead of the term 'cross-frontier' insurance, within the European Community such activities are referred to as 'services' insurance.

2. Although the *Convention on Jurisdiction and the Enforcement of Judgments* was agreed by the original member countries in 1968 and was amended in 1973 to accommodate Denmark, Ireland and the United Kingdom, it finally came into effect in January 1987.

3. The Commission intend to issue in 1991 a Recommendation to encourage all member states to regulate insurance intermediaries.

4. Report prepared for the Commission of the European Community by Carter and E.V. Morgan, *Freedom to Offer Life Insurance Across EEC State Boundaries* (London: Economists Advisory Group, 1986).

Chapter 8

Prospects for Freer Trade in Insurance

THE PROSPECTS for the liberalization of trade in insurance will be considered in this chapter in the context of the two main international fora — the Organization for Economic Co-operation and Development (OECD) and the General Agreement on Tariffs and Trade (GATT). The progress which has taken place within these bodies is reviewed. Finally, some views are advanced on the main obstacles that are likely to be faced in future trade negotiations on insurance in the multilateral arena, with some suggestions how these obstacles might be circumvented at least in part.

DISCUSSIONS WITHIN THE OECD

Introduction

The OECD was formed in 1960, having evolved out of the Organization for European Economic Cooperation (OEEC) which had been set up 12 years earlier to assist in the post-war process of rebuilding the economies of Europe under the Marshall plan. Since its inception, recognition of the importance of global economic interdependence has been central to the philosophy of the OECD, a key aspect of which has been to encourage governments to adopt policies aimed at greater trade liberalization and greater freedom of international capital movements.

The membership of the OECD has always been small, currently consisting of 24 of the leading industrialized nations. Its size, combined with the relative cohesiveness of economic outlook of its members, has allowed it to discuss contentious issues in a broad and integrated way. Nevertheless, it cannot be said to represent a global perspective, since it does not allow explicitly for the views of developing and newly industrialized nations.

Within the OECD, freedom for insurance transactions and the related issues of international payments and capital flows are governed by three general instruments of liberalization. There are two sets of competition rules which have been periodically updated since their introduction in the early 1950s: the Code of Liberalization of Current Invisible Operations and the Code of Liberalization of Capital Movements. In 1976 these Codes were supplemented by the National Treatment Provisions of the Declaration and Decisions on International Investment and Multinational Enterprises. Together these instruments capture the major facets of international insurance trade, both on a cross-frontier and establishment basis.

Broadly speaking, the underlying aim of the two Codes and the 1976 Declaration is to extend to individuals and corporations resident in one member country the freedom to transact business or invest in another member country in the same way that exists for residents within an individual country, with the freedom extending to payments associated with these transactions.

Although it has its own nomenclature, the OECD operates under similar principles to those used within GATT, viz. national treatment, non-discrimination, transparency and progressive liberalization. Technically, the Codes are decisions of the OECD Council and are formal international agreements that are binding on the adhering countries. There is no obligation to liberalize under a Code immediately, but rather there is a commitment to a progressive liberalization over time. Those members which are unable to liberalize immediately are permitted to lodge a *reservation* (or an *exception* under the National Treatment Instrument) on the particular liberalization item. Member countries that wish to lodge a reservation must give reasons for their actions and there is a periodic examination of these reservations to prevent countries from dragging their feet.

Although decisions of the OECD Council are legally binding on member countries, there exist no effective enforcement mechanisms. In practice, this often limits the ability of the OECD to convert good intentions into real action.

Earlier Attention to Insurance

From its early days, the OECD has had a specialist Insurance Committee with a membership which has included insurance practitioners and regulators. Within the financial services sector, this committee is unique. Its origin dates back to the earlier OEEC days. Its role arose in part because many insurance transactions have been historically international in character, with their obvious links to trade in goods, and in part to the fact that insurance has long been subject to a wide variety of complex restrictions which demanded a technical competence to interpret clearly.

A principal responsibility of the Insurance Committee has been to assist the Committee on Capital Movements and Invisible Transactions (CMIT) to update the insurance section of the Invisibles Code and to undertake periodic examinations of members' reservations under the Code. Because of its membership, it has been called on from time to time to assist in a wide variety of technical matters relating to insurance.

Meetings of the Insurance Committee, while fairly frequent in the 1950s and early 1960s, lapsed until the mid-1970s. One reason for this was a reluctance on the part of some of the member countries from the European Community to consider any wider initiative until insurance liberalization within the Community had been achieved. Moreover, it was considered by some members that harmonization of supervisory control must precede any detailed liberalization discussions.

In 1972 the high-level group on trade and related problems, which was established the year before the OECD Council to advise governments on the development of international economic relations, devoted a few pages to the subject of services in its report on policy perspectives.[1] The group, under the chairmanship of Jean Rey, formerly a President of the European Commission, urged that action should be taken by the developed countries to ensure liberalization and non-discrimination in the services sector. In the field of insurance the Rey Report recommended the following.

'Insurance probably deserves first attention not only because of its economic significance, but also because more than elsewhere progress towards real liberalization is held up by involved technical arrangements. The rules of the Code of Liberalization of Current Invisible Operations concerning direct insurance transactions are incomplete and there are, moreover, numerous reservations on liberalized operations (including insurance relating to goods in international trade), because the authorities of a number of member countries are opposed to liberalization as long as there is no international harmonization of national insurance control regulations. These countries maintain that without such harmonization, conditions of international competition would be distorted. This is disputed by other member countries which have in fact liberalized without ill-effects. The advantages for trade and industry of a progressive liberalization of the international insurance market are such, not least in the context of inflation, that the question should be re-examined with some urgency.'

This call for liberalization was reinforced in a report by an advisory group of the Trade Policy Research Centre, in London, under the chairmanship of Sir Frank McFadzean (the McFadzean Report)[2] which appeared concurrently with the Rey Report in 1972.

Even so, in 1974 and 1975 the Council for Ministers of the OECD, influenced by the then OECD Secretariat, gave serious thought to abolishing the Insurance Committee because of its failure to achieve any results. From the mid-1970s onwards, however, the importance of trade in services in general, and trade in insurance in particular began to be recognized.

Pioneering work[3] of the Trade Policy Research Centre in London, of the International Chamber of Commerce and of individuals, particularly Brian Griffiths and Ronald Shelp (who was for a while Vice-President of the major US insurer, American International Group) helped to develop a wider political awareness. Political interest had been built up to such an extent that the OECD Council of Ministers instructed the Committee for Capital Markets and Invisible Transactions (CMIT) in 1980 to begin a major update of the Current Invisibles Code to make it a more effective instrument for the liberalization of international service operations. And at a more general level, the Council also encouraged the Committee on Trade and Related Problems to begin to investigate the obstacles to trade in services in a more systematic way.

More Active Discussions in the 1980s
This changed political climate prompted the Insurance Committee to become much more active than it had been in the past. A joint working group of the CMIT Committee and the Insurance Committee was set up to look at the restrictions and problems encountered in international insurance transactions and to examine ways of achieving a greater liberalization. The first task of the joint working group was to obtain greater transparency of government policies in member countries and to make a detailed survey of restrictions on international insurance operations. It was also asked to assess the relative importance of these restrictions and their effects on insurance operations; this proved to be too ambitious a task at the time. The report on this first phase of the work, which was published in 1983, stated:[4]

'International insurance activities may take the form of international rendering of services, which correspond, in the area concerned, to international trade in goods or they may be carried out in the form of services provided by subsidiaries or branches of foreign insurers established in a given country. The proportion of international activities carried out in the latter form is larger in the insurance sector, as perhaps in other service sectors, than in the case of trade in goods. This is due to the fact that in the insurance sector, it is often necessary that foreign concerns be established in a country to be able to offer their services on a competitive basis in that country's market.

'Obstacles exist to both forms of international insurance activities mentioned above. Without attempting to classify these obstacles in a strict order of importance, it may well be said that the most serious impediments — those which affect most significantly enterprises willing to engage in international activities — concern establishment in terms of both number of restrictions and degree of severity.'

In their final report the joint working group put emphasis on the question of access to insurance markets and stressed that attempts to reduce restrictions on establishment should be given the first priority. It could be argued that the report did not pay sufficient attention to the particular problems that Lloyd's of London and the insurance exchanges in the United States and elsewhere face, because their organizational structures do only easily permit them to supply international insurances on a cross-frontier basis.[5] It is, however, relevant to point out that Lloyd's of London and these insurance exchanges have still been able to grow rapidly in recent years because they had been able to access international insurance markets through reinsurance, which has been relatively free of restrictions.

The Council of Ministers gave the Insurance Committee a wider mandate in the mid-1980s. The Committee was again asked to assist the CMIT in its updating of the insurance section of the Current Invisibles Code and its periodic invitations to governments to justify their reservations against implementing the Code. However, because of the need to deal with establishment issues in a more systematic way than previously, it was considered necessary to also address matters which were technically within the Capital Movements Code and the National Treatment Provision of the 1976 Declaration, such as the formation of local subsidiaries, joint ventures and take-overs. A further *ad hoc* working group of the CMIT and Insurance Committees was set up in 1987 to carry out an in-depth study of the motivations behind what were perceived to be the more severe restrictions and discriminatory tax policies pertaining to cross-frontier insurance transactions.[6] This study was completed in 1989.

During the 1980s major changes were also made in the Capital Movements Code.[7] In 1984 it was significantly extended to ensure a comprehensive coverage of all the main aspects associated with the right of establishment and related direct investment issues. The Capital Movements Code was further extended in 1989 to embrace all short, medium and long term capital transactions. These extensions of the Capital Movements Code had significant implications for the insurance industry not only with regard to establishment but also in respect of their cross-frontier business, since some aspects of international life insurance and fund management transactions were covered within the Capital Movements Code.

In addition to the work related to updating of these Codes, the Trade Committee of the OECD increased its activity from the early 1980s onwards. This was due in part to the increasing political interest among a number of member countries regarding trade in services, not least because of the more overt efforts to introduce services within the GATT. A number of governments felt that the OECD might prove an alternative forum in which to pursue trade liberalization discussions on services should attempts to bring such discussions into GATT fail. With this in mind, the Trade Committee developed a framework of analysis within which trade in services could in principle be assessed. This framework was completed in 1986.[8] The OECD Secretariat was also asked to try to apply the analytical framework to the major service sectors. One of the first reports from the Secretariat dealt with insurance. The report was completed in the latter part of 1986 and entitled

Sectoral Study on the Relevance of the Conceptual Framework: Insurance.[9] The Insurance Committee of the OECD was not formally involved in writing the report, but it did provide the OECD Secretariat with the necessary technical information to complete its study.

Conclusions

While it is true to say that actual progress in achieving greater liberalization in insurance with the OECD has been limited, its most useful role has been as a forum in which the key areas of concern have been identified and the differences of opinion among its members have been exposed. From time to time there have been heated debates, especially between the United States and a number of countries in the European Community on this scope for further liberalization of cross-frontier insurance business, fairer modes of establishment and more balanced regulatory systems. The fact that the location for the meetings of the Insurance Committee has been in Paris has also assisted in this. It has helped European countries to respond more freely to US assertiveness, while the concurrent experience within the EC to try to create a common market in insurance has also assisted in informing the debates.

The benefits of these open exchange of views are hard to ascertain. It is possible that external pressure from the United States on some of the more conservative members of the Community to adopt a more liberal stance with regard to cross-frontier business will bear fruit in time, and indeed assist the EC in its own aims in this area. But there is no doubt that the United States has come to realize that there is a need to address issues back home, not least the question of the piecemeal state regulation that exists there, possibly with the long-term aim of moving towards a single licence principle similar to that planned for the European Community. There is a case for aguing that these pressures have contributed in part to the more liberal stance evident in Japan in recent years, which has resulted in the Ministry of Finance granting a

limited number of licences to foreign insurers, which previously
had been virtually impossible to secure.

DISCUSSIONS WITHIN THE GATT

Introduction

Since 1948, the GATT has been the principal multilateral
body which has sought to lay down principles and rules
governing the conduct of international trade. The underlying
philosophy of the GATT is that liberal trade is beneficial to
global economic growth and fair trade is an essential basis for
the conduct of international commerce. Evidence of its broad-
based support is provided by the fact that at the time of writing
107 countries, both developed and developing, have become
signatories to the GATT and participate in its negotiations.
In the face of an endemic tendency in many countries to seek
the short-term benefits of economic protectionism, the GATT
has provided a forum within which negotiations have taken
place, guided by a clear set of principles based on non-
discrimination (most favoured nation), national treatment and
reciprocity.

Compared with the OECD, its main advantages as a forum
for trade negotiations has been that it has a much broader
representation of countries and has well-tested protocols and
procedures for hammering out compromises, with a system
for settling disputes. On the other hand, its terms of reference
are narrower, and the size and diversity of its membership
make it more difficult to arrive at a consensus.

Until the Uruguay round, attention in the seven previous
rounds of negotiations have focussed solely on trade in goods.
Failure to include trade in services explicitly in the negotiating
framework can be traced in part to the failure of government
policy world-wide to appreciate earlier the growing importance
of services as a source of economic growth and employment.
But since the mid-1970s, there been an increasing
recognition of the role of services and attempts to move
economic policy away from its traditional emphasis on goods.

This has led governments, sometimes prompted by sectoral commercial interests, to seek to extend negotiations on trade issues to include services.

Since GATT had already proved itself to be an effective body in which to conduct trade negotiations in goods, there was a sound case for bringing any future negotiations on trade in services into the same forum, or at least within its ambit, rather than to seek to create a new body.

Although insurance *per se* had not yet reached the formal agenda of the GATT, some discussions had been carried out at a less formal level. Between 1953 and 1959 there were investigations by the GATT Secretariat into the question of discriminatory practices with respect to insurance of cargoes in transit. A report, following an enquiry by the Secretariat in 1954, found:

(a) that discriminatory practices were prevalent in certain countries, mainly developing countries; and

(b) that there were some *prima facie* evidence of the harmful effects of those practices on the flow of international trade in goods.

But the general outcome from the discussions was that the issue was neither sufficiently important nor conclusive to warrant the drafting of a specific international convention or an amendment to the General Agreement. A concurrent study by the Internatonal Monetary Fund found that only a few countries deployed their exchange-control machinery to restrict payments to foreign insurers arising from the supply of transport insurance cover. The issue was the subject of further discussion in 1955 and 1959; although support was voiced in principle for freer competition, recognition was given to the ambitions of those developing countries wishing to build up their own local insurance markets and no action ensued.[10]

These early initiatives on insurance were taken by the United States in response to submissions by the International Chamber of Commerce. It is interesting to note that these arguments in support of the liberalization of insurance trade were based on the indirect effects on trade in goods and not the direct effects on insurance as an industry in its own right.

US Initiative to Bring Services into GATT

After the conclusion of the Kennedy Round negotiations in 1967, the signatory countries to the GATT agreed to the compilation of an inventory of discriminatory non-tariff measures which distorted international trade. The inventory contained a number of notifications relating to services. As the governments were beginning to think about another round of GATT negotiations, a high-level group in the less formal context of the OECD drew attention to the need to deal with restrictions in the services sector.

In the United States, services were specifically included within the Trade Act of 1974 following pressures from representatives of the service industries including insurers. This was a significant development in that the Trade Act provided the basis of the US Administration's negotiating authority for the Tokyo Round of negotiations. More importantly for the future, it precipitated the setting up of a high-level inter-agency task force, the chairman of which came from the US Department of Commerce, to look at how services might be introduced into multilateral trade negotiations.[11] In its report, published in late 1976, the task force recommended that service-industry trade problems should be raised in the Tokyo Round negotiations on a carefully selected basis, focussing on those problems which were similar to the goods-related non-tariff measures already scheduled for discussion.[12] 'A longer term objective in raising services in the multilateral trade negotiations', the task force argued 'should be to put our trading partners on notice that greater attention will be paid to services in future negotiations.'

An already full agenda and insufficient background research meant that little systematic discussion on trade in services could take place in the Tokyo Round negotiations. But the United States indicated that it wanted consultations on the following:

(a) the requirement by Argentina that insurance must

be placed with a national insurance firm;

(b) the requirements in Colombia that 60 per cent of reinsurance should be placed locally;

(c) the requirement in Venezuela that 40 per cent of reinsurance should be placed locally;

(d) the requirement in Nigeria that insurance should be placed with Nigerian-registered insurance companies; and

(e) the requirements in Romania and Poland that foreign trading organizations should use the national insurance monopoly for insuring exports.

It was apparent to the United States delegation, and indeed to other parties, in the negotiations that discussions on these issues could not take place at that time, especially as the items raised represented only a few examples of the restrictions that existed in member countries. Their introduction was meant to give a clear signal that the United States intended to raise the question of restrictions of trade in insurance and in other service industries during future negotiations of the GATT.

It was at the GATT ministerial meeting in November 1982 that the United States proposed that the GATT should look at the question of incorporating service industry transactions, including insurance, in future negotiations. The United States was supported in its efforts by the United Kingdom. Many of the other developed countries were not initially enthusiastic about this proposal, partly because they had not had time to consider the implications of such a change on their own national positions. A number of developing countries, led by India and Brazil, were flatly opposed to it. It was agreed without commitment, however, that the feasibility of including trade in services might be considered later. It was proposed that individual countries with an interest in trade in services should first produce national studies on the barriers to trade in services and give their general assessment for progress in this direction. Not surprisingly, the first national study submitted came from the United States. The United States study recognized that if services were to be included within the GATT, amendments to the existing GATT articles would be needed, though many of them could be extended to embrace services. It was also argued that no liberalization of trade in services could disregard direct investment issues, and insurance was recognized as being one of the services where establishment issues must be addressed. In the words of the study:

'The thrust of efforts internationally should be to obtain perhaps through an agreement on insurance, acceptance of the principle of the right of access to domestic markets, subject to adherence to legitimate local regulatory requirements. 'Access' would mean basically the right to sell policies within the guidelines established earlier in the study dealing with trade and investment. A multilateral arrangement might commit governments to establish guidelines that ensure fair and equitable access to local markets, taking into account the sovereignty of domestic regulatory procedures. Once access is gained, national treatment would be the operative principle.'[13]

Even so, a cautionary note was added:

'If countries are to embark on the formulation of trade rules for services, they must know whether this can be done in a meaningful way without dealing with the more sensitive issue of investment in services.'[14]

Following the completion of other national studies, the United States, Canada, the European Community, Japan and a number of other developed countries agreed to address the question of how they could introduce services into a new round of GATT negotiations. As the United Kingdom had been fully aware of the United States initiative from the outset and had developed its own national position, it acted as an important agent in encouraging the other Community countries to support the attempt to introduce services within the GATT.

The strong initial opposition by a number of developing countries to attempts to begin any discussion on services within the GATT reflected their perception that the primary motivation for the initiative arose from a narrower commercial interest on the part of the proposing countries. Moreover, and perhaps more importantly, these developing countries did not perceive any benefits to themselves from such negotiations. Consequently a small group of developing countries sought to frustrate attempts to get negotiations on services started, on the grounds that the GATT did not have the legal authority to embrace them.

Progress Within the Uruguay Round

In spite of these objections, it was agreed at the Punta del Este (Uruguay) ministerial meeting held at the end of September 1986 that a new round of GATT negotiations should commence and that there should be an attempt to bring trade in services into the negotiating framework. The procedural compromise which gained majority support for this proposal was that a special group would be set up, the Group of Negotiations on Services (GNS), which would investigate how GATT principles and protocols could be applied to trade in services.

Tactically, it was thought necessary in order to secure agreement to proceed with talks about talks and to keep the discussions separate from the main GATT negotiations, even though there would be every effort to adhere to GATT principles. This kept open the possibility for negotiations on trade in services to be brought together with those goods in the long-term or, at least, if they were to remain separate, they could be run side-by-side in future rounds of negotiations, hence allowing for bargaining between the two to take place.

Since the GNS had a voluntary membership, it was considered important to seek to attract as many countries as possible into these preliminary talks. It was also decided that there should be an attempt to include as many commercially traded services as possible, in part in the interests of comprehensiveness and in part to increase the chances of enlarging the membership of GNS, since some countries, particularly developing countries, might only have an economic interest in a limited number of service industries.

It was also considered expedient to adopt a less structured and gradualist approach to the talks: to explore concepts and principles and to avoid discussing detailed or technical matters which might cause the talks to drift towards well-entrenched negative positions. Central to the approach was that the discussions should deal with matters affecting all services and leave until later those germane to specific sectors. But it was recognized by all parties that trade in a number of service sectors would imply market access through some form of establishment.

This low key approach proved successful, as was evident from the fact that a number of developing and newly industrialized countries decided to join the GNS. Even India and Brazil, which had been strongly opposed to such negotiations earlier, felt that it was in their longer term interest to be party to the talks. This involvement of the less developed countries was formalized by the appointment of Felipe Jaramillo, a Colombian, as chairman of the GNS.

Work on widening the number of service sectors to be covered continued. A list of 13 service sectors was produced including 340 different service activities.

In December 1988, when the mid-term review of the GATT negotiations were held in Montreal, the GNS was able to put forward some well thought out aims and principles for consideration. The major elements of these are well summarized by Brian Woodrow below:[15]

• provisions to promote *transparency* of domestic and international laws, regulations and administrative practices to services;

• a commitment to *progressive liberalization* as a general principle and its application in some agreed form to specific services sectors, with acknowledgement of the particular difficulties of its application to developing countries;

• *national treatment* for services exports and or exporters of signatories vis-a-vis domestic services or services providers in the same market;

• where *market access* is made available, foreign services may be supplied according to the "preferred mode of delivery";

• *Most-Favoured-Nation Treatment/non-discrimination* should apply in that benefits should be extended to all signatories and apply equally to all services covered;

• *increasing participation of developing countries* should be encouraged through enhanced market access for services exports of developing countries with specific reference to improved access to distribution channels and information networks and possible special treatment for the least-developed countries;

• *safeguards/exceptions* are recognized as possibly necessary for dealing with adverse temporary circumstances or for reasons of a more permanent nature;

• acknowledgement of the right of countries to continue to regulate their services sectors, where they feel it appropriate, but recognition that asymmetries exist in the *regulatory situation* of different countries and that any introduction of new regulations should be consistent with country commitments to progressive liberalization under the framework.

In the remaining two years up to the planned completion of the Uruguay round in December 1990, the GNS set itself two main tasks. First, it wished to be in a position to put forward a General Agreement on Trade in Services covering all the agreed sectors. Second, it intended to have ready separate annexes which identified particular liberalization considerations facing the major service sector groups.

Insurance was to be included along with banking and investment services in an annexe for the financial services sector as a whole. This contrasted with its earlier positioning, where insurance had often been advanced as the *cause célèbre* for seeking to liberalize trade in services. A lower profile for insurance was welcomed by the insurance industry. The more liberal, and hence often the more active, insurance industry interests recognized the benefit of having a broad bridgehead in order to obtain the maximum political momentum behind the initiative. The coupling of insurance with the banking and investment was also acceptable. This was not only because a number of issues associated with trade in banking and investment services are similar to those in insurance but also because life insurance companies supply investment services and deal in securities. Moreover, there was a recognition among a number of European members that experience with attempts to create a common market in insurance in the EC had benefited from the more rapid progress on the liberalization of banking, in particular the single licence principle that was planned to be the centre piece of the Insurance Framework Directives had come directly from the Second Banking Directive.

Even though there were attempts to avoid areas of contention, the negotiations within GNS were not free of disagreement. Countries with more liberal intentions queried the need to extend the same degree of benefits to those countries which were likely to be less willing to make similar commitments. Indeed for a short while there was some pressure from the US Treasury to try to take banking services out of the negotiations, on the grounds that prudential supervision might be compromised by horse-trading that might accompany any agreement. Developing countries also emphasized the need for a slower adjustment for themselves and disputes arose on some aspects of the market access issue, fearing that their local service industries would need much more time to withstand the force of international competition.

By the time of the December meeting in 1990, which was scheduled to close the GATT round, a General Agreement on Trade in Services (GATS) had been prepared, although it contained a large number of qualifications. And not all the sectoral annexes were available for tabling; more particularly, no financial services annexe was ready, due to differences in opinion, especially between the developed and developing countries, and to the complexity of the technical issues involved. However, it was the long standing dispute over agricultural subsidies that caused the failure of the round to be completed on time.

Hopefully, an agreement will be reached by the end of 1991. This will afford more time to clarify further the General Agreement on Trade in Services and to complete the financial services annexe. In addition, it will also allow individual countries more time to decide on what initial commitments they will offer to liberalize immediately, which has been made a precondition of being a signatory to the GATS.

But it has been evident that progress on liberalizing trade in services within the GATT context will be a long and drawn-out process. This will come as no surprise to the insurance sector which has been involved in the protracted discussions within the OECD and, for some, within the European Community for many years. What is seen as being more important is that the agreement must have a broad consensus and be sufficiently robust to last into the next century.

Conclusions

It would seem appropriate to conclude the study by identifying what are the main obstacles that are likely to surface in future negotiations on insurance within the GATT framework. Some suggestions are also offered which it is hoped will help to circumvent these obstacles.

First, the Group of Negotiations on Services, or its successor, must adhere to the policy that developing countries should be allowed to liberalize progressively, at a slower rate than the more developed countries. Since the developed countries have been the most keen to bring services into the multinational framework, they should lead by example. While developing countries are responsible for many of the restrictions and barriers to the free flow of international insurance and reinsurance, the developed countries also impose restrictions on international insurance transactions. Cross-frontier direct insurance is severely restricted in a number of European countries, and also in Japan. Even in the United States which has a comparatively free market some restrictions exist at the state level which inhibit the flow of certain types of insurance, in particular "surplus" line business. Regulatory issues may be at the heart of many of these restrictions, but there are protectionist elements to be found in them too. Discriminatory practices with regard to establishment also exist in a number of developed countries. Hence it is reasonable to suppose that only when the developing countries see some significant progress being made in these established markets will they be inclined to think that liberalization is not just a means of allowing the larger insurance companies from these markets to expand their international business interests. As negotiations proceed, it may well prove beneficial for a two or three speed system to be set up. But if this is the case, sufficient incentives will have to be built in to discourage developing countries from liberalizing at too slow a pace.

Particular problems face developing countries that have insurance industries that are nationalized. National treatment is not the problem here, since indigenous private sector companies are also prevented from competing. What is required is to encourage a more general liberalization of economic and commercial policy. There are signs that a number of these countries are abandoning their state-control philosophies and beginning to see the benefit of attracting private foreign capital and know-how.

At the same time there should be more political will placed behind the initiatives within the OECD to achieve greater liberalization among its membership. Liberalization within the OECD is consistent with a two speed approach. The Insurance Committee should be encouraged to continue to clarify issues relating to insurance in a broad and unconstrained way, perhaps working more closely with committees representing other financial services interests, and to provide signals about particular areas of difficulty to the wider multilateral forum so that these can be avoided in the negotiation process. Some formal link should exist between OECD and GATT to ensure that these signals are sent and received.

Second, the issue of market access is likely to prove a contentious issue in future negotiations. Recognition in the General Agreement in Trade in Services (GATS) that services may be supplied according to a preferred "mode of delivery" is important for insurance. Different types of insurance have different preferred modes of delivery. Reinsurance, marine, aviation and transport insurances and insurances on large scale projects often need to be conducted on a cross-frontier basis, not least because of a commercial imperative to spread risk. Indeed this also applies to the direct insurance requirements of large firms, especially multinational firms. On the other hand, insurances for individuals and small to medium-size businesses, both life and non-life, normally require delivery through a local establishment.

Effective freedoms for cross-frontier business also have to take into account the role of intermediaries. Insurance brokers, loss adjusters and other major insurance intermediaries require freedom to operate so as to facilitate these international insurance and reinsurance transactions. They are the conduit through which much of the cross-frontier business flows and to perform their role, and to be able to provide adequate on-the-spot service, they often also require a right of establishment.

Negotiators should recognize that commercial preferences do not always conflict with regulatory and wider government preferences. While a minimum establishment for a foreign insurance supplier is a local agency with the binding authority to write business on its behalf, in many situations foreign insurance companies would prefer, or at least would not be unduly averse to, establishment in the form of a local company. This is because operating through a local company affords a commercial benefit in that it conveys to potential local consumers the appearance of a permanent presence which is important in insurance, since security is a key product characteristic. In many cases, the initial capital and on-going operating costs of setting up a local company are not significantly greater than that of a branch, although ill-thought out regulation can sometimes make them so. What is more important to foreign insurers is lack of national treatment, which makes it more difficult for them to compete fairly with locally-owned enterprises. To be more precise, it is equivalent treatment that is the concern, since foreign insurance companies have to service their suppliers of capital and often need to integrate their local reinsurance protections into wider reinsurance treaty arrangements, hence equivalent treatment usually demands the concomitant freedom to transfer funds abroad.

Third, a major potential constraint on liberalizing insurance transactions, and indeed other financial service transactions, will be regulatory stances. In the first place, negotiators will have to discriminate carefully between the various purposes behind national legislation. The only universally justifiable purpose for regulation is consumer protection.

In addressing these legitimate regulatory concerns, it will be advisable to have both a short and a long-term goal. In the long-term, the solution that is planned for introduction in the European Community would appear to be best, namely, to move towards a single licence system. Under such a system, insurers supplying insurances on a cross-frontier basis or on an establishment basis through agencies and branches are subject to a regulatory control only in their home country; whereas insurers supplying through a local subsidiary or joint venture, the regulatory control in the host country applies. For such a system to operate, there has to be a minimum yet adequate set of agreed solvency and compensation standards, which can be applied globally, as well as mutual recognition, trust and co-ordination between supervisors.

In the late seventies, the authors recognized this regulatory stumbling bloc to progress on trade liberalization in insurance. At the time we proposed as a solution that an international solvency standard should be set up, the main purpose of which would be to allow a supervisor in one country to delegate responsibility for regulation to supervisors in others. We envisaged that direct insurers and specialist reinsurers should be subject to the same solvency standard, although there would clearly have to be different criteria for life insurance and for non-life insurance because the characteristics of these two broad classes of business are not the same. This proposal was broadly similar to the single licence principle that has subsequently emerged within the European Community. But there is one lesson that the subsequent European experience has shown, which we did not sufficiently recognize at the time: to effect real progress there must be an emphasis on the concept of regulatory equivalence. In other words, regulatory and associated compensation systems can differ, providing they meet certain minimum standards. Acceptance of regulatory equivalence avoids the lengthy process of searching to harmonize legislation which can seriously frustrate the liberalization process.

But there will also need to be a shorter-term solution to the regulatory problem in a complex multilateral setting to prevent negotiations from stalling. Inevitably, short-term solutions entail compromise. The following compromise is proposed. Cross-frontier business should be subject solely to home country control, while all forms of establishment, whether through an agency, branch, subsidiary or joint-venture should be subject to host country control, i.e. they would be regulated by the supervisory authority in the country of their establishment. This would simply extend the regulatory practice that exists for a local subsidiary under the single licence principle to all forms of establishment. It would require regulatory systems in a number of countries to move gradually away from their traditional emphasis of host country control towards accepting some form of home country control as well. A worldwide list of approved insurers and reinsurers, derived from a model for solvency assessment to which supervisors and market participants also supplied information, would help to underpin the confidence of supervisors in their acceptance of a system entailing the principle of more home country control.

There would be nothing to prevent groups of countries, such as those within the EC, from moving quickly towards the more progressive single licence principle among themselves. The evolution towards a single licence might be through regional groupings, such as the EC, or it could emerge more quickly if it were to be adopted by all the members of the OECD.

The above discussion still begs the key question what are the areas of insurance for which full liberalisation should be sought in any forthcoming negotiations i.e. where the insurers would be free to supply insurances internationally using any mode of delivery they choose, and where consumers are given similar freedoms to buy. We suggest that modest targets should be aimed for, at least initially, given the difficulties experienced on this matter within the EC, which have still not yet been resolved in practice. It would be sensible to only seek to negotiate initially for this wider liberalisation in those areas where there already exists a good deal of market and regulatory freedom. We would propose that this is limited to reinsurance transactions and direct insurances relating to marine, aviation, transportation insurances and large-scale projects. Even within these fields there is still plenty of scope for the reduction of restrictions.

For all other areas of insurance, we would suggest that the right of market access should be limited to a local establishment. Moreover, the chances of success in future negotiations are likely to be even higher if this right is restricted to the formation (or the agreed acquisition) of a local company. This is because supply through a local company would yield the best compromise between the various interests: those of insurance companies, those of supervisors, those of government economic policymakers, and not least those of consumers. Of course, this would be a minimum right of access, and individual countries could, and indeed should be encouraged to, extend this right to all modes of access, which is the long term aim.

NOTES AND REFERENCES

1. *Policy perspectives for International International Trade and Economic Relations* (Rey Report), High Level Group on Trade and Related Problems (Paris): OECD Secretariat, 1972 pp. 77-80.

2. Sir Frank McFadzean, *et al.*, *Towards an Open World Economy, Report of an Advisory Group*, (London: Macmillan, for the Trade Policy Research Centre, 1972). The members of the advisory group were Sir Frank McFadzean (Chairman), Sir Alec Cairncross, Professor W.M. Corden, Mr Sidney Golt, Professor Harry G. Johnson, Professor James Meade and Mr T.M. Rybczynski.

3. Brian Griffiths, *Invisible Barriers to Invisible Trade*, (London: Macmillan, for the Trade Policy Research Centre, 1975): Ronald K. Shelp, 'The Proliferation of Foreign Insurance Laws: Reform of Regression', *Law and Policy in International Business*, No. 8 1976 and *Beyond Industrialization: Ascendancy of the Global Service Economy*, (London: Praeger, 1981).

4. 'International Trade in Services: Insurance — Identification of Obstacles' *op. cit.*, p 10.

5. Not all the business of Lloyd's of London is carried out on a cross-frontier basis. Lloyd's has limited establishments in the form of appointed local representatives in Kentucky and Illinois and in a number of European countries. Moreover, it also does so by virtue of its granting to the overseas branches and subsidiaries of insurance brokers a limited form of establishment in foreign markets binding authority to accept risks exists.

6. *Motivations for existing OECD restrictions on the conclusion of insurance contracts with non-residents and restrictive effects of existing discriminatory tax measures*, (Paris: OECD Secretariat, 1987) Private circulation.

7. M.F. Houde 'Building International Services Trade Policies at Agreements: OECD Instruments' Applied Services Economic Centre (ASEC) in *Proceedings of 2nd International Services Forum on Global Services and Trade Liberalization* (Geneva) May 21-22, 1991.

8. *Conceptual Framework for Trade in Services*, (Paris: OECD Secretariat, 1986) Private circulation.

9. *Sectoral Study on the Relevance of the Conceptual Framework: Insurance*, (Paris: OECD Secretariat, 1986) Private circulation.

10. See R.J. Krommenacker, *The Liberalization of Invisible Trade and the Inclusion of Services in GATT Negotiations: The Case of Transport Insurance* (Geneva Association Internationale pour l'Etude de l'Economie de l'Assurance, 1976).

11. The task force drew mainly on the study on services by Brian Griffiths, *op. cit.*

12. See *United States Service Industries in World Markets: Current Problems and Future Policy Development*, Task Force on Services and the Multilateral Trade Negotiations (Washington: Department of Commerce, 1976).

13. *US National Study on Trade in Services* (Washington: Office of the US Trade Representative, 1983) p.228.

14. *Ibid.*, p. 8.

15. R. Brian Woodrow, Implications for Major Services Sectors and International Business in *Uruguay Round Trade in Services Perspectives*, Proceedings of the 1st International Forum on Global Services and Trade Liberalization, Applied Services Economic Centre, (Geneva) May 15-17 1990.

16. R.L. Carter and G.M. Dickinson. Barriers to Trade in Insurance. Thames Essay No. 19. London: Trade Policy Research Centre, 1979 p68. See also Carter and Dickinson 'Economic Effects of Restrictions on Trade in Reinsurance. Proceedings of the 3rd R.O.A. Seminar, Cambridge, 1977, p52.

Appendix I

Restrictions on International Business

GOVERNMENT legislation and practices vary widely among countries in their impact on international insurance and reinsurance and can be subject to rapid change. It is not possible in an essay such as this to provide a detailed list of restrictions as they existed at the date of writing, which apply to both insurance transacted on a cross-frontier basis and through local establishment. The countries listed in Table A.1 and Table A.2, therefore, are those with the largest insurance markets within the main regions of the world, excluding the centrally-planned economies.

The information has been compiled from many national and other sources, including R.M. Crowe (ed.), *Insurance in the World's Economies* (Philadelphia: Corporation for the Philadelphia World Insurance Congress, 1982) and *International Trade in Services: Insurance — Identification and Analysis of Obstacles* (Paris: OECD Secretariat, 1983).

TABLE A.1

Restrictions on International Insurance — Cross-frontier Basis

Country	Limitations on placing insurance abroad (excluding reinsurance)	State-owned reinsurance company	Compulsory reinsurance cessions to state reinsurer or local market	Restrictions on remittances by consumers, ceding insurers or reinsurers	Restrictions on contract enforceability and servicing	Localization of funds (including 'gross reserving' in reinsurance)	Discriminatory taxation
Federal Republic of Germany	Yes[d]	No	No	No	Yes	Yes	No
United Kingdom	No	No	No	No	No	No	No
France	Yes	No	No	Yes	Yes	Yes	No
Netherlands	No	No	No	No	No	Yes	No
Italy	Yes	Yes	Yes	Yes	Yes	Yes	No
Switzerland	Yes	No	No	No	Yes	Yes	No
Sweden	No	No	No	Yes	No	Yes	No
Belgium	Yes	No	No	No	No	Yes	No
Japan	Yes	Yes[a]	Yes[b]	No	Yes	Yes	Yes[c]
India	Yes	Yes	na	na	na	na	na
Iran	Yes	Yes	Yes	Yes	na	na	na
Republic of Korea	Yes	Yes	Yes	Yes	No	Yes	nk
Philippines	Yes	Yes	Yes	Yes	Yes	Yes	nk
Taiwan	Yes ·	Yes	Yes	No	nk	nk	nk
Malaysia	Yes	Yes	Yes	Yes	Yes	Yes	No
United States	Yes	No	No	No	No	Yes	Yes
Canada	No	No	No	No	No	Yes	Yes

South Africa	Yes	No	Yes	nk	Yes	Yes
Nigeria	Yes	Yes	Yes	Yes	Yes	No
Egypt	Yes	Yes	nk	na	na	na
Kenya	No	No	Yes	No	Yes	nk
Algeria	Yes	Yes	na	na	na	na
Morocco	Yes	Yes	Yes	nk	nk	nk
Israel	Yes	No	Yes	No	Yes	nk
Iraq	Yes	na	na	na	na	na
Turkey	Yes	Yes	Yes	No	Yes	nk
Saudi Arabia	No	No	No	No	No	Yes
Brazil	Yes	Yes	Yes	No	Yes	nk
Argentina	Yes	Yes	Yes	Yes	Yes	Yes
Mexico	No	Yes	No	nk	Yes	nk
Venezuela	No	Yes	No	Yes	Yes	Yes
Columbia	Yes	Yes	Yes	Yes	Yes	nk
Peru	Yes	Yes	Yes	nk	nk	nk
Australia	Yes[d]	No	No	No	No	Yes
New Zealand	Yes[d]	No	No	No	No	Yes

[a] For earthquake risks only.
[b] Compulsory automobile liability insurance and earthquake insurance only.
[c] Unless official approval is granted.
[d] Restrictions on involvement of intermediaries

na — not applicable.
nk — not known.

TABLE A.2

Restrictions on International Insurance — Local Establishment Basis

Country	Industry totally nationalized	Local incorporation mandatory	Local shareholding required	Discriminatory licensing restriction	Restrictions on employment of overseas personnel	Restrictions on profit remittances	Discriminatory taxation
Federal Republic of Germany	No	No	No	Yes	No	No	No
United Kingdom	No	No	No	Yes	No	No	No
France	No	No	No	Yes	No	No	Yes
Netherlands	No	No	No	Yes	No	No	No
Italy	No	No	No	Yes	No	Yes	No
Switzerland	No	No	No	Yes	Yes	No	No
Sweden	No	No	No	Yes	No	No	Yes
Belgium	No	No	No	Yes[a]	No	No	No
Japan	No	No	No	Yes	nk	No	nk
India	Yes	na	na	na	na	na	na
Iran	Yes	na	na	na	na	na	na
Republic of Korea	No	No	Yes	Yes	nk	Yes	nk
Philippines	No	No	Yes	Yes	Yes	Yes	nk
Taiwan	No	No	No	Yes[b]	Yes	nk	nk
Malaysia	No	Yes	Yes	Yes	Yes	Yes	nk
United States	No	No	No	No	No	No	No
Canada	No	No	No	No	No	No	Yes

South Africa	No	Yes	Yes	Yes[b]	Yes	Yes	Yes
Nigeria	No	Yes	Yes	Yes	Yes	Yes	nk
Egypt	Yes	Yes[c]	Yes	Yes	Yes	Yes	nk
Kenya	No	Yes	Yes	Yes	Yes	Yes	nk
Algeria	Yes	na	na	na	Yes	na	nk
Morocco	No	Yes	Yes	Yes	Yes	Yes	Yes
Israel	No	No	No	No	No	Yes	nk
Iraq	Yes	na	na	na	na	na	nk
Turkey	No	No	No	Yes	No	Yes	nk
Saudi Arabia	No	No	No	No	No	No	nk
Brazil	No	Yes	Yes	Yes	Yes	Yes	Yes
Argentina	No	Yes	No	Yes	Yes	Yes	nk
Mexico	No	Yes	Yes	Yes	Yes	No	nk
Venezuela	No	Yes	Yes	Yes	Yes	Yes	nk
Columbia	No	Yes	Yes	Yes	Yes	Yes	nk
Peru	No	Yes	Yes	Yes	Yes	Yes	nk
Australia	No	No	No	Yes	No	No	Yes
New Zealand	No	No	No	Yes	No	No	nk

[a] For branches.
[b] No new foreign companies allowed (other than American in Taiwan)
[c] Free Zone established where joint foreign/Egyptian companies may be formed.

na — not applicable.
nk — not known.

GATT Recommendations on Insurance Transactions

THE following paragraphs reproduce the GATT recommendations on insurance transactions; both are concerned with transport insurance.

DRAFT RECOMMENDATION FOR ELIMINATION OF RESTRICTIONS IN REGARD TO TRANSPORT INSURANCE[1] (1955)

Taking note of the Resolution of the United Nations Economic and Social Council at its fifteenth session (Resolution 468 H [XV] of 16 April 1953) and of the Studies and Reports of the Secretary-General of the United Nations and of the Executive Secretary of the CONTRACTING PARTIES on restrictive measures in regard to transport insurance and their effect on international trade.

Considering that measures adopted by certain countries which restrict the freedom of buyers and sellers of goods to place transport insurance on the most economic basis create, in certain circumstances, obstacles to international trade in that they increase costs of goods entering into international trade.

Recognizing that progressive elimination of such restrictive measures will facilitate the expansion of international trade; and

Recognizing further that most countries regulate the activities of insurance firms operating on their territory and that national regulation of such activities which addresses itself to the solvency, reliability, prudence and legal accountability of particular firms does not itself constitute an interference to the freedom of traders in the transport insurance field and therefore does not of itself create obstacles to international trade;

THE CONTRACTING PARTIES

Recommend that governments should avoid measures in regard to transport insurance which have a more restrictive effect on international trade than those they now apply and should move as rapidly as circumstances permit to reduce any restrictive measures currently in force with a view to their eventual elimination;

Request governments to report to the Executive Secretary any information relevant to the subject matter of this Recommendation not previously reported to him, including the steps they have taken to eliminate measures contrary to the purpose of this Recommendation.

FREEDOM OF CONTRACT IN TRANSPORT INSURANCE: GATT
RECOMMENDATION OF 27 MAY 1959[2]

Taking note of the resolution of the United Nations Economic and Social Council at its fifteenth session (resolution 468 H [XV] of 16 April 1953) and of the studies and reports of the Secretary-General of the United Nations and of the Executive Secretary of the CONTRACTING PARTIES on restrictive measures in regard to transport insurance and their effect on international trade;

Considering that measures adopted by certain countries which restrict the freedom of buyers and sellers of goods to place transport insurance on the most economic basis create, in certain circumstances, obstacles to international trade in that they increase costs of goods entering into international trade;

Recognizing that most countries regulate the activities of insurance firms operating on their territory and that national regulations of such activities which addresses itself to the solvency, reliability, prudence and legal accountability of particular firms does not itself constitute an interference to the freedom of traders in the transport insurance field and therefore does not of itself create obstacles to international trade; and

Taking note of the desire of countries that do not have a sufficiently developed and effective national insurance business to take such measures as they consider necessary to foster such a business;

THE CONTRACTING PARTIES

Recommend that in the formulation of national policies in the field of transport insurance, governments should endeavour to avoid measures that would have a restrictive effect on international trade,

Recommend that this matter be regarded as a subject of interest to the CONTRACTING PARTIES, and

Request governments to report to the Executive Secretary any information relevant to the subject matter of this recommendation not previously reported to him.

REFERENCES

1. Draft recommendations, L/462, drafted at the Tenth Session of the Contracting Parties in November 1955 (Geneva: GATT Secretariat, 1955).

2. GATT recommendations of 27 May 1959, *Basic Instruments and Selected Documents*, 8th Supplement (Geneva: GATT Secretariat, 1959) p. 26.

Towards a Common Insurance Market in Europe

THE following is a summary of developments in insurance trade within the European Community largely extracted from a paper prepared by the Association of British Insurers' International Committee.[1]

INTRODUCTION

When the European Economic Community was established in 1957, certain general principles were laid down in the Treaty of Rome by the original six states, including the attainment of the following objectives which are of relevance to the creation of a common insurance market:

(a) the abolition, as between Member States, of obstacles to freedom of movement for persons, services and capital;

(b) the institution of a system ensuring that competition in the common market is not distorted;

(c) the application of procedures by which the economic policies of Member States can be coordinated and disequilibria in their balances of payments remedied; and

(d) the approximation of the laws of Member States to the extent required for the proper functioning of the common market.

More specifically, the Treaty laid down a 12-year timetable for the introduction of freedom of establishment and services for insurance. By freedom of establishment is meant the right of nationals of all Member States to set up an agency, branch

or subsidiary anywhere in the Community including the right
'to take up and pursue activities as self-employed persons and
to set up and manage undertakings, in particular companies
or firms ..., under the conditions laid down for its own
nationals by the law of the country where such establishment
is effected'. Freedom of services, on the other hand, would
allow insurers to provide cover from an office in one Member
State for risks of other Member States without having an
establishment there.

Freedom of establishment and services were to be achieved
by means of directives which, *inter alia*, were intended to
abolish restrictions on freedom of establishment and services
and approximate the laws of the Member States 'to the extent
necessary for the proper functioning of the common market'.
A timetable was laid down for the introduction of the two
freedoms in stages during a transitional period; this provided
for freedom of establishment and services for reinsurance by
the end of 1963 and freedom of establishment and services
for non-life and life insurance by the end of 1969. Freedom
of services for non-life and life insurance was to be conditional
on prior introduction of freedom of establishment,
simplification of procedures for reciprocal enforcement of
judgments and coordination of insurance contract law. The
first two have now been achieved by the Non-Life and Life
Insurance Establishment Directives and the Convention on
Jurisdiction and Enforcement of Judgments, but it has not
been possible to reach agreement on coordination of insurance
contract law. The Non-Life and Life Insurance Services
Directives therefore allow only limited choice of law, and the
draft Non-Life and Life Framework Directives maintain these
limitations, with greater freedom of choice being provided only
for non-life "large risks" as defined by the Non-Life Services
Directive.

Unfortunately, it was not found possible to keep to the
original timetable. Although reinsurance presented few
difficulties, directives on freedom of establishment for non-life
and life insurance were not agreed until 1973 and 1979

respectively, with the Non-Life Services Directive following in 1988 and the Life Services Directive in 1990. In a number of important European Court of Justice cases in the early 1970s (in particular the Reyners and Van Binsbergen cases), it was held that freedom of establishment and services had existed since the end of the transitional period, i.e. from the beginning of 1970. However, court cases deal only with specific questions and directives coordinating rules and regulations are still necessary in order to facilitate these freedoms and to clarify the basis on which business can be written.

There was a gradual resurgence of political pressure for completion of the internal market in the early 1980s, which led to the EC Commission producing a White Paper entitled "Completing the Internal Market" in June 1985. This White Paper, which was endorsed by the Council of Ministers, identified the various barriers to a free market and set out a programme of some 300 directives aimed at their removal. The intention was that these directives should be implemented by 1992; although the timetable has not been adhered to and the Commission are now hoping to see the main directives adopted by that date.

In November 1989 Sir Leon Brittan announced a radical new approach consisting in the introduction of the single licence approach, whereby all the activities of insurers will be subject to the control essentially of the home country supervisory authorities, with the existing distinctions between large and mass risks largely being swept away. Under this approach, to be implemented by the draft Non-Life and Life Framework Directives, the operations of insurers in their own country, through branches in other countries and by way of services business will come under the control only of the home country authorities as regards financial aspects (solvency and technical reserves), with the host country retaining some influence as regards compulsory insurance but in general being able to apply only its rules "in the general good" to the operations of foreign insurers through branches in their country and by way of services business.

This radical new approach, which has already been adopted for the banking sector, will, if not introduced with restrictions to remove much of its effect, introduce a genuine common market, though it will in practice take time for individuals to become accustomed to the idea of going outside their own country for their insurance cover. The availability of advice from independent intermediaries will be essential if consumers are to make use of the new freedoms, and the Commission are encouraging those markets which do not currently regulate intermediaries to do so by means of a Recommendation (to be published during 1991) laying down basic standards for intermediaries.

EC Directives in Force (as at June 1991)

Reinsurance

Directive 64/225, on freedom of establishment and services in the field of reinsurance and retro-cession, abolished restrictions based on nationality on the freedom of individuals and companies to establish and provide services in reinsurance. Where an individual or a company is also engaged in direct insurance, that part of the business is excluded from the provisions of the directive.

Non-Life Establishment

This directive, number 73/239, relates to freedom of establishment for direct non-life insurance, and was issued in parallel with directive 73/240 (the so-called "Suppression Directive") which removed restrictions on freedom of establishment for this type of insurance. The directive was intended to facilitate freedom of establishment by coordinating the conditions relating to the taking up and pursuit of direct non-life insurance by undertakings whose head offices are situated within the Community and by agencies or branches of third country undertakings. The former must be officially authorised, adopt particular legal forms, submit a scheme of operations, hold certain technical reserves and maintain a solvency margin and guarantee fund. Branches and agencies of third country undertakings must be entitled to carry on insurance business under their own national law and must keep separate accounts, hold local reserves and maintain a solvency margin and guarantee fund.

Life Establishment

This directive, number 79/267, is the equivalent for life insurance of the Non-Life Establishment Directive. It contains similar provisions to that directive, and also provides that pre-existing composite companies (transacting both life and non-life business) can continue, subject to rules on separate management, with a review of the operation of composite companies to be undertaken after ten years (as a result of this review, which was concluded in early 1991, the Commission have included provisions in the draft Life Framework Directive — see paragraph 4 below — to remove all restrictions on composite insurers, on the grounds that there is no evidence to suggest that policyholders are any more at risk if they take out a policy with a composite insurer than if the policy is taken out with a specialist insurer). The requirements of the directive were due to come into force by September 1981, with transitional periods (generally five years) for compliance with requirements regarding solvency margins and the separate management of the life and non-life business of composite insurers.

Insurance Intermediaries

This directive, number 77/92, is intended to facilitate practical exercise of freedom of establishment and services, by laying down objective standards of training, experience and good repute which the regulating authorities in a member state must accept as sufficient qualification for nationals from other member states to practise there. In the UK, insurance brokers are governed by the Insurance Brokers (Registration) Act 1977.

The directive will be supplemented by a Recommendation to be issued by the Commission during 1991 which is intended to encourage those member states that do not already regulate insurance intermediaries to do so.

Community Coinsurance

Directive 78/473 was intended to create true freedom of services in coinsurance (where a risk is covered by more than one insurer), as a first step towards freedom of services in non-life insurance as a whole. The risks to be freed were those "which by reason of their nature or size are liable to be covered by international coinsurance". In practice, little use has been made of the directive because of differences of view as to whether the leader must be established in the country of the risk and as to the meaning of "nature or size".

The Commission instigated proceedings against France, Denmark, Ireland and Germany for including requirements in their legislation implementing the directive whereby the leader had to be in the country of the risk and community coinsurance was only possible for risks above a certain size in terms of thresholds. The European Court ruled that the leader can be based in any member state but also acknowledged the validity of monetary thresholds as a criterion for determining which risks were suitable for community coinsurance.

Freedom of Services for Non-life Insurance

This directive, number 88/357, is the second step (the Coinsurance Directive having been the first step) towards freedom of services for non-life insurance. The directive introduces a freer regime for "large risks", with other ("mass") risks still being subject largely to the control of the host country.

One part of the directive supplements the Non-Life Establishment Directive, in particular by incorporating in that directive a definition of "large risks" (marine, aviation and transport insurance, credit and suretyship insurance in the case of professional, industrial or commercial policyholders, and property, general liability and miscellaneous financial loss above thresholds which will be halved from 1.1.93).

Another part deals specifically with freedom of services and provides that "large risks" can be written on a services basis subject only to various details including solvency being provided to the supervisory authority of the country of the risk. As regards "mass" risks, member states may require administrative authorisation before allowing undertakings from other member states to provide cover on a services basis for risks in their territory (only the UK and Netherlands have decided not to require such authorisation).

Greece, Ireland, Spain and Portugal have been allowed transitional arrangements for implementing the freer regime for large risks. The other member states should have fully implemented the directive by the end of June 1990, but some have yet to introduce the necessary legislation and the Commission have announced that they will be instigating proceedings against these countries. In the meantime, the Commission have said that insurers are still free to write large risks business in those countries, despite the directive not having been implemented.

Motor Insurance

Directive 72/166, known as the "Green Card" Directive, together with associated supplementary agreements, abolished the checking of green cards at frontiers between EC member states and other countries which agreed to implement the provisions of the directive. Policies must give the minimum compulsory cover in all the countries which apply the directive.

A second directive on third party motor insurance, number 84/5, was adopted at the end of 1983. This supplemented the 1972 directive, as follows:-

(a) Compulsory insurance must cover not only bodily injury but also property damage;

(b) Liability must be covered up to certain minimum limits;

(c) Compensation must be guaranteed up to the

minimum limits in the case of uninsured or unidentified vehicles;

(d) insurers must not exclude members of the family of the policyholder, of the driver or of any other person responsible for the accident from the cover they give.

The directive had to be implemented by the end of 1988 but longer periods were provided for Greece, Ireland and Italy.

A third directive on motor insurance adopted on 14th May 1990, number 90/232, is intended to resolve certain problems arising in some of the member states which result from or were left unresolved by the first and second directives on motor insurance.

The first aim is to ensure that all passengers, other than the driver and passengers who have knowingly and willingly entered a stolen vehicle, should be covered for personal injury by compulsory third party insurance. The second aim is to implement fully the objective of the first directive that all third party motor insurance policies should provide at least the minimum cover required by law in all the member states, which was not the position in Italy and Greece. The directive must be implemented by 31st December 1992, but transitional arrangements apply to Greece, Ireland, Spain and Portugal.

Legal Expenses Insurance

This directive, number 87/344, was adopted in June 1987 and removes the provision in the Non-Life Establishment Directive that allows Germany to maintain its system of compulsory specialisation for legal expenses insurance. The text is based on a compromise solution which allows specialist and composite insurers to operate side by side subject to the safeguards of free choice of lawyer for the insured, separate management and accounting by composite companies writing this class and the ability for member states to require composite companies to channel legal expenses claims through a separate organisation (in this context, ''composite'' means writing more than one kind of non-life insurance). The free choice of lawyer for the insured is intended to reduce to a minimum the possibility of conflicts of interest where a policyholder has more than one policy, e.g. legal expenses and motor, with the same company.

The directive came into force at the end of June 1990.

Credit Insurance

This directive, number 87/343, is similar to the legal expenses insurance directive in that it abolishes the specialisation requirement in Germany for credit and suretyship insurance. The text contains additional safeguards for credit insurance, these being mainly additional financial requirements. It is provided that insurers must keep separate accounts and maintain a higher guarantee fund than previously, and insurers are required to set up equalisation reserves for the purpose of offsetting any technical deficit or above-average claims ratio. Export credit insurance "for the account of or guaranteed by the state, or where the state is the insurer" is excluded pending further coordination.

Assistance

This directive, number 84/641, brings assistance activities within the scope of the 1973 Non-Life Establishment Directive as a new class 18. It provides for freedom of establishment of undertakings wishing to carry out assistance business and lays down a framework for member states to supervise the financial soundness of these undertakings by requiring the maintenance of solvency margins and permitting checks to be made on their resources. The directive had to be in force by January 1988.

Capital Movements

A directive was adopted in November 1986 and another in June 1988 relating to liberalisation of capital movements. These directives amended the previous, 1960, directive by removing several of the exemptions in that directive which had meant that the practical effects were very limited. The 1960 directive liberalised "transfers in performance of insurance contracts'', i.e. premiums and payments in respect of life assurance, premiums and payments in respect of credit insurance and other capital transfers in respect of insurance contracts. These provisions related only to premiums and claims, not the capital of insurance companies. The 1986 directive liberalised movements of capital in respect of unit trusts and other mutual funds and also the purchase and sale of unlisted securities.

As part of the completion of the internal market, the aim of the 1988 directive is to remove controls on all capital movements by 1992. It entered into force in eight member states on 1st July 1990, but Greece, Ireland, Portugal and Spain were allowed transitional arrangements.

Jurisdiction and the Enforcement of Judgements

A Convention on Jurisdiction and the Enforcement of Judgements was agreed by the original six member states in 1968 and - amended following the accession to the EC of Denmark, Ireland and the UK in 1973. The Convention lays down common rules of jurisdiction and standardises the procedures for obtaining enforcement of judgements. There is a special section on insurance dealing with the courts in which insurers can be sued and agreements on jurisdiction between insurers and policyholders. The amended Convention has only been in effect from 1st January 1987, following its ratification by all six original member states and one of the other member states.

UCITS

Directive 85/611/EEC of 20th December 1985 (as amended by 88/220/EEC of 22nd April 1988) on the coordination of laws, regulations and administrative provisions relating to undertakings for collective investment in transferable securities (UCITS) came into force on 1st October 1989, although Greece and Portugal were allowed to defer implementation until 1992.

The purpose of the directive is to enable investment products falling within the scope of the directive to be promoted and sold throughout the Community. The directive applies only to unit trusts which are open-ended and which invest principally in transferable securities listed on recognised stock exchanges. Other types of unit trusts, commonly referred to as non-UCITS, are not covered.

DIRECTIVES ADOPTED BUT NOT YET IN FORCE
Freedom of Services for Life Insurance
This directive, number 90/619, was adopted on 8th November 1990 and must be in force in the member states by 20th May 1993.

The directive supplements the Life Establishment Directive of 1979, in particular as regards choice of law, transfers of portfolios between different insurance companies, and reciprocity with third countries. It also contains provisions relating to freedom to provide services, and in this connection distinguishes between passive (own initiative) business, where the proposer takes the initiative in approaching an insurer in another country, and active business, where the insurer actively seeks business in other countries.

Unlike the Life Establishment Directive, the directive does not apply to certain types of business including pension fund management.

Like the Non-Life Services Directive, the directive provides a freer regime for risks where the policyholder is deemed to require less protection, but in this directive the distinction is not between large and mass risks but between own initiative and active business. For own initiative business, insurers are only required to notify the host country of their intention to write the business, and approval of rates and conditions by the host country is not allowed for such business. For active business member states can require insurers to be authorised by the host country and can also require rates and conditions to be approved. Composite insurers (writing both life and non-life business) are permitted to write own initiative business and also active business if permitted at the time the directive is notified in a particular member state and in the other member states until 31st December 1995 (the Commission proposes to remove the restrictions under this directive and the Life Establishment Directive by means of a provision in the draft Life Framework Directive).

The Directive allows Greece, Spain and Portugal to restrict services business to own initiative business for certain periods and to apply their own legislation to technical reserves during these periods. The Directive also provides the following options for all the member states:-

— prohibition of own initiative business, until 31.12.94, in respect of group insurance contracts entered into by virtue of the insured person's contract of employment or professional activity;

— prohibition of use of local intermediaries for own initiative business, for up to three years from the coming into force of the directive (until 20th May 1993).

Freedom of Services for Motor Insurance

This directive, number 90/618, was adopted on 8th November 1990 and must be in force by 20th November 1992. The directive deletes the exclusion of motor third party liability insurance in the Non-Life Services Directive and also includes motor insurance in the "large risks" regime of that directive. This means that risks above the thresholds already applicable to the property classes will benefit from the more liberal regime applicable to large risks, while other risks will, like other "mass" risks, be subject to administrative authorisation by the country of the service.

However, various aspects of the greater freedom regarding technical reserves for "large" motor risks are deferred as follows:-

(a) *calculation* of the technical reserves is placed under the supervision of the host state until the directive co-ordinating the annual accounts of insurance undertakings *comes into force*;

(b) the covering of these reserves by *equivalent and*

matching assets is placed under the supervision of the host state until the *notification* of the Third Non-Life (Framework) Directive *comes into force*;

(c) the assets representing the technical reserves are to be *localised* in the host state until the third Non-Life (Framework) Directive *comes into force*.

The directive also requires insurers writing motor insurance on a services basis to become members of the national Bureau and national Guarantee Fund of the country of the service. The member state of the service may require an insurer to nominate a local representative to be responsible for the handling and settlement of claims. The existence of such a representative cannot be deemed to equate to a branch or agency and will therefore not require the insurer to be established in the country of the service.

DRAFT INSURANCE DIRECTIVES

The main draft directives which directly affect insurance are as follows:-

Draft Non-Life Framework Directive

The initial draft of this directive was adopted by the Commission in July 1990 and the Commission hope that it can be adopted at the end of 1991, to come into force at the end of 1993. The directive will introduce the single licence for non-life business, which means that the head office supervisor of an insurer will be responsible for the financial aspects of regulation (solvency margin and technical reserves) not only in respect of the head office but also as regards branches in other countries and cross-border ("services") business.

In addition, the directive contains the following provisions:
— because it has not been possible to reach agreement on the draft Insurance Contract Law Directive, the Commission have given up the idea of coordinating insurance contract law and have instead retained the choice of law provisions of the 1988 Non-Life Services

Directive. These are based on the principle of the country
of risk law applying for mass risks. However, the complete
freedom of choice of law allowed for marine, aviation and
transport insurance has been extended to "large risks"
as defined by the Non-Life Services Directive.

— abolition of approval of rates and conditions.
Instead, it is proposed that there should be non-systematic
notification of conditions to the host country supervisor
after the insurer has started to write business there, with
advance systematic notification for compulsory insurance
and health insurance issued as a substitute for social
security.

— freedom to localise technical reserves anywhere in
the Community, and greater relaxations as regards
matching of the assets representing the technical reserves,
with the ability to match 100% in ECU.

— harmonisation of cover for technical reserves on the
basis of a fairly extensive list of permitted assets and with
member states not being able to require investment in
particular types of asset.

Draft Life Framework Directive
The initial text of this directive was agreed by the
Commission on 20th February 1991. Most of the provisions
are virtually identical to those in the Non-Life Framework
Directive, but the draft has additional provisions for life
insurance covering the following:-

— actuarial principles for calculating technical reserves
based on proposals by the EC Consultative Group of
Actuaries;

— disclosure of information to the policyholder before
the contract is signed and also during the term of the
contract;

— a cooling-off period of 14-30 days. This now applies
to establishment business (the Life Services Directive
introduced it for services business only);

— matching rules similar to those for non-life insurance

in the Non-Life Services Directive but with a new provision relating to unit-linked contracts;

— provisions lifting the restrictions on composite insurers in the Life Establishment and Life Services Directives.

Draft Insurance Accounts Directive

This draft directive covers the layout of the balance sheet and profit and loss accounts and contains rules for the valuation of assets. It is considered to provide sufficient harmonisation for non-life insurance as regards the definition and calculation of technical reserves, but the draft Life Framework Directive supplements this directive by provisions on calculation of technical reserves for life insurance.

Proposed Insurance Committee

The EC Commission propose to set up a new Insurance Committee and, for this purpose, published a draft directive in July 1990. The Committee would be responsible for operating the reciprocity rules in the insurance sector and also for technical work such as occasional adaptations to the rules governing the composition of technical reserves. In addition, the Commission would like the Committee to develop an advisory function, acting as a forum where there could be discussion of general policy issues affecting the insurance sector and allowing the national supervisory authorities to develop close ties and closer working relationships.

OTHER DRAFT DIRECTIVES

Proposed Pension Funds Directive

It was originally thought that the management and provision of pensions by life insurers would come under this directive, but it has now been decided that pensions managed and provided by life insurers will come under the Life Framework Directive. The Pension Funds Directive therefore applies only to supplementary occupational or professional schemes provided by non-insurance financial institutions (including non-insurance subsidiaries of insurance companies). Personal pensions will come under the life Framework Directive as far as insurance companies are concerned, with those provided by other institutions coming under the Second Banking Directive, draft Investment Services Directive and the UCITS (unit trusts) Directive as appropriate.

A first draft of the directive is expected in mid-1991. It is intended to implement the following three freedoms:

— freedom to manage pension funds anywhere in the Community;

— freedom to invest pension fund assets freely across national frontiers;

— freedom to establish pension funds at a European level, to which groups of workers in different member states could belong. These pension funds would not have uniform rules but would take account of rules in each country, as it would not be practicable in the short term to overcome the difficulties that exist as regards taxation and employment laws.

Draft Investment Services and Capital Adequacy Directives

The Investment Services Directive is intended to introduce the single licence for investment firms. Insurers are seeking to have tied agents excluded from the directive, on the grounds that their principals (i.e. insurance companies) will be responsible for them and that separate authorisation is therefore not required.

The Capital Adequacy Directive supplements the Investment Services Directive by laying down initial capital requirements for investment firms, including intermediaries who sell and advise on investments.

Insurance Intermediaries

The Commission intend to issue a draft Recommendation during the first half of 1991. This would not be binding on member states but is intended to encourage those member states which do not regulate insurance intermediaries to do so, given that access to sound financial advice is of importance for consumers wishing to take advantage of the new freedoms being introduced by insurance directives which will allow them to take out insurance anywhere in the Community.

COMPETITION POLICY

One of the objectives of the European Community is the institution of a system ensuring that competition is not distorted. The Directorate-General within the Commission responsible for competition has, since the early 1980s, turned its attention to insurance agreements and their compatibility with the provisions of the Treaty of Rome. In 1984 Directorate-General for competition gave exemption to the agreement of an Italian machinery-breakdown pool. The original agreement was said to restrict competition between the companies that were members of the pool and also restrict members' choice of reinsurers. The exemption, for ten years, was given only after changes to the agreement had been accepted. They included a change from a commercial to a pure premium tariff (that is, without a loading for expenses) and the removal of a restriction whereby reinsurers had agreed not to grant more favourable reinsurance terms or premiums on the Italian market outside the pool.

Another agreement granted exemption for ten years by Directorate-General for competition, from 1985, was the International Group Agreement of the marine Protection and Indemnity (P and I) Clubs. The exemption, as with the Italian agreement, followed the agreement of the P and I Clubs to make various changes to their agreement in order to allow greater possibilities for competition between clubs in respect of premiums.

Arguably the most important case, with wider implications, is that relating to premium recommendations issued by the German Property Association (GPA) in 1980 in relation to fire and consequential loss insurance. In December 1984, the Directorate-General for competition gave a decision whereby they refused an application by the GPA for negative clearance of the recommendation and the Germans subsequently appealed against that decision. The Commission argued that Article 85 of the Treaty of Rome was applicable to insurance and that trade between Member States was affected by the recommendations because branches in the Federal Republic of Germany of non-German companies within the Community were members of the GPS and parties to the premium recommendations. A ruling by the European Community Court of Justice was given on appeal on 27 January 1987 and this decision upheld the earlier decision of the Commission. In particular, the Court ruled as follows:

That Articles 85 and 86 of the Treaty of Rome apply without restriction to insurance and that the only sectors to which the competition rules in those articles do not apply are those sectors expressly exempted by the Treaty of Rome. This application without restriction of the competition rules does not, however, mean that the Commission is unable to take into account the special features of any particular sector under Article 85 paragraph 3.

Even though the recommendations were not obligatory, they should be considered as a decision in the meaning of Article 85 given that they had a stated, precise aim which involved influencing the behaviour of the Association's members.

Contrary to the views of the GPA, which said that the recommendations were merely the result of normal and necessary technical cooperation and had not in any event been followed in practice, the Court held that the actual effect of an agreement was irrelevant if the aim was to restrict competition as was the case here.

The Court rejected the argument of the Association that the recommendations did not affect trade between Member States. The fact that only branches of foreign companies in the Federal Republic of Germany were affected by the recommendations did not prevent financial relations between a branch and its parent company being affected, whatever the degree of legal independence of the branch. At the time of the Commission decision German legislation was very restrictive as regards the activities of foreign undertakings. Nevertheless, these companies could still participate in German insurance operations by setting up a branch or taking part in coinsurance. The recommended increases in premiums, which did not take into account the individual situation of insurers, were likely to affect the position of foreign insurers capable of offering a more competitive service.

The Association had said that an exemption was justified because the recommendations aimed to re-establish the profitability of insurers while safeguarding the interest of the insured. The Court pointed out that the Commission had the task, when considering its decision, of deciding whether the recommendations contributed to the improvement of insurance services and whether the recommendations went beyond what was necessary to achieve this effect. The Court said that because of the general scope of the recommendations and lack of differentiation between different companies, the increases related not only to claims costs but also the administrative expenses of insurers which differed widely between one company and another. The global nature of the increases was therefore of a kind to restrict competition in a way going beyond what was necessary.

Following representations from the insurance industry, in 1991 a Regulation was adopted enabling the Commission, after consulting the Advisory Committee on Restrictive Practices and Monopolies, to issue a Regulation exempting certain types of cooperation agreements between insurance undertakings and associations. The Regulation can apply to such matters as common risk premium tariffs based on collective statistics, standard policy covers and conditions, and the settlement of claims. Within six years of such a Regulation being brought into force a report on its functioning will have to be presented to the European Parliament and the Council.

REFERENCE

1. 'Progress Towards the EC Single Market in Insurance', I/515/231, British Insurers' International Committee, London, March 1991.

Insurance Spending and Economic Development

IN CHAPTER 1 it was noted that insurance spending in developing countries has grown significantly during the last decade. In this appendix an attempt is made to analyze briefly the relationship between insurance spending and the level of economic development. Gross domestic product (GDP) per head is used as a measure of the level of economic development.

In Figure AIV.1 below we hypothesize the relationship that might be expected to exist between insurance spending per head and GDP per head. At low levels of economic development spending on insurance would be low because both insurable wealth and financial awareness are limited and because the opportunity cost of making provision to replace assets is high. As economies continue to develop, the business sector expands, personal wealth grows and financial awareness increases, all of which is conducive to increased spending on insurance. Indeed, insurance spending per head might be expected to grow faster than GDP per head above a certain level of development. As economies mature, insurance spending is likely to continue to increase but at a relatively slower rate: there must be an upper limit on the proportion of a country's GDP that is spent on insurance.

Individual countries will differ in their propensity to insure as they progress through different stages of economic development. Differences in demography and in the political and socio-cultural environment will have major effects, particularly on life insurance.[1]

Attention will be focussed on the following:

(a) A cross-sectional analysis of the relationship between insurance spending per head and of GDP per head for a sample of developed and developing countries during 1988.

(b) A temporal analysis of the changes in insurance spending per head to GDP per head between 1978 and 1988 for a sample of developing and developed economies.

FIGURE AIV.1

Insurance Spending and GDP per Head

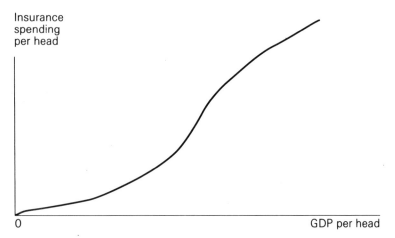

INSURANCE DATA

Data on insurance spending for individual countries is collated annually by the Swiss Reinsurance Group. This information is published each year in the April or May issue of its monthly publication, *Sigma*. A breakdown is given of the insurance spending in each market between life and non-life insurance. Over the years the Swiss Reinsurance Group has sought to increase the number of national insurance markets that are covered. The April 1990 issue of *Sigma* provides data coverage for 56 countries in 1988, if one excluded the centrally planned economies. The data available for both 1978 and 1988 is limited to 42 countries.

INSURANCE SPENDING AND GDP: A CROSS-SECTIONAL ANALYSIS

First let us look at the cross-sectional relationship between insurance spending and GDP for 1988. There is a separate analysis for life insurance and for non-life insurance, because the determinants of demand will differ significantly for each.

To test the relationship between these two variables, a regression model of the following form is used:

$$\log P_j = \log a + b \log G_j + \log e_j$$

where P_j = gross premiums per head for country j in 1988

G_j = GDP per head for country j in 1988

The regression findings are given below, with the standard errors of the parameter estimates given in brackets.

Non-life Insurance

$$\log P_j = -2.95 + 1.31 \log G_j$$
$$(0.42) \quad (0.05)$$
$$\bar{R}^2 = 0.93$$
$$DW = 1.72$$

Life Insurance

$$\log P_j = -3.96 + 1.51 \log G_j$$
$$(1.15) \quad (0.14)$$
$$\bar{R}^2 = 0.69$$
$$DW = 2.51$$

These cross-sectional relationships are well-defined, especially for non-life insurance. In both regressions, the parameter b is significantly greater than 1, thus indicating insurance spending for life and non-life per head grew at an increasing rate relative to that of GDP per head. It will be noted that the exponential rate is higher for life insurance than for non-life insurance.

Attempts were also made to investigate whether some levelling off in the rate of increase in insurance spending at high levels of GDP could be discerned from the data by fitting a variety of non-linear functional forms. The findings, which are not reported here, were inconclusive.

Temporal Changes in Insurance Spending and GDP

Additional, and perhaps more meaningful, insights into the relationship between insurance spending and GDP can be obtained by analysis over time. To test whether growth in insurance spending over the 10 year period 1978 to 1988 differs with the level of economic development, a simple model of the following form suggests itself.

$$\Delta P_j = a + bG_j + e_j$$

where ΔP_j = percentage change in gross premiums per head
for country j between 1978 and 1988

G_j = average level of GDP per head during period 1978 to 1988

Regressions were fitted for changes in the level of life and non-life insurance spending over this 10 year period against the average level of GDP during this 10 year span. The data exhibited a pattern, but the pattern could not be captured to a statistically significant degree in the fitted regressions because of major variations in the growth of insurance spending between countries with a similar level of GDP per head.

Nevertheless, the pattern in the data is displayed in Table AIV.1 below. The 42 countries are ranked in the order of their average level of GDP per head during the 10 year period and then consolidated in 7 ranked groups of 6 countries each.

For each of these groups the percentage change in the ratio of insurance spending to GDP between 1978 and 1988 is calculated for life and for non-life insurance.

TABLE AIV.1

Countries ranked in terms of average level of GDP per head over 1978/1988 period	Percentage change in the ratio of insurance spending to GDP between 1978 and 1988			
	Non-life Insurance		Life Insurance	
	Unweighted mean	Unweighted standard deviation	Unweighted mean	Unweighted standard deviation
	%	%	%	%
Group 1 (highest)	10.4	18.4	46.7	24.2
Group 2	18.0	21.3	84.2	64.6
Group 3	15.6	21.1	59.3	35.1
Group 4	37.2	35.2	221.3	301.0
Group 5	22.9	26.6	166.9	202.2
Group 6	15.9	24.4	52.1	71.9
Group 7 (lowest)	11.8	33.6	21.6	35.9
All 42 countries	18.8	27.8	93.2	158.6

As can be seen, the overall growth of life insurance spending relative to GDP is much greater than that for non-life over this period. The unweighted overall mean is 93.2% for life insurance compared with 18.8% for non-life insurance over the 10 year span, although the variation between countries is relatively higher for life insurance. This is a similar finding to the cross-sectional analysis presented earlier.

Of more significance is the pattern between the 7 groupings. It can be seen that both for life and non-life, countries in the middle range of GDP per head exhibit the fastest growth, even though the variations within these groups are greater than those for the higher or lower groups. Furthermore, countries with the lowest GDP per head have the lowest relative growth

List of References

THIS list contains only the more important references cited in the text. The reader should refer to the Notes and References at the end of each chapter for more complete bibliographical information.

A.Z.A. ALI, *Insurance Development in the Arab World* (London: Graham & Trotman, 1985).

P.C.I. AYRE, 'The Future of Private Foreign Investment in Less Developed Countries' in T.J. Byrne (ed.) *Foreign Resources and Economic Development* (London: Frank Cass, 1972).

J.S. BAIN, *Barriers to New Competition* (Cambridge, Massachusetts: Harvard University Press, 1956).

TONY BAKER, 'Liberalization and Reinsurance Interests', *Policyholder*, Stockport, 15 April 1983.

ROBERT E. BALDWIN, *Non-tariff Distortions to International Trade* (Washington: Brookings Institution, 1970).

R.E. BEARD, 'The Three Rs of Insurance — Risk, Retention and Reinsurance', *Journal of the Institute of Actuaries Students Society*, London, Vol. 15, Pt. 6, 1959.

M. BEENSTOCK, GERARD M. DICKINSON and S. KHAJURIA, 'Determination of Life Premiums: an International Cross-section Analysis, 1970-81', *Insurance: Mathematics and Economics*, Amsterdam, Vol. 5, 1986.

B. BERLINER, *Limits of Insurability of Risks* (Englewood Cliffs, New Jersey: Prentice Hall, 1982).

DAVID L. BICKELHAUPT and RAN BAR-NIV, *International Insurance: Managing Risk in the World* (New York: Insurance Information Institute, 1983).

ROBERT L. CARTER, *Economics and Insurance* (Stockport: P.H. Press, 1972).

ROBERT L. CARTER, 'Further Comment on Insurance and Development', *Best's Review*, Oldwick, New Jersey, April 1976.

ROBERT L. CARTER, *Reinsurance* (Brentford, Middlesex: Kluwer Publishing, 1983).

ROBERT L. CARTER and GERARD M. DICKINSON, 'Economic Effects of Restrictions on International Trade in Reinsurance', Proceedings, 3rd International Reinsurance Conference, Reinsurances Offices Association, Cambridge, 1977.

ROBERT L. CARTER and NEIL DOHERTY, 'Tariff Control and the Public Interest', *Journal of Risk and Insurance*, Bloomington, Illinois, September 1974.

RICHARD E. CAVES and R.W. JONES, *World Trade and Payments* (Boston, Massachusetts: Little, Brown, 1973).

G. CLAYTON and W.T. OSBORNE, *Insurance Company Investment* (London: Allen & Unwin, 1965).

W.M. CORDEN, *Trade Policy and Economic Welfare* (Oxford: Oxford University Press, 1974).

R.M. CROWE (ed.), *Insurance in the World's Economics* (Philadelphia: Corporation for the Philadelphia World Insurance Congress, 1982).

GERARD M. DICKINSON, *International Insurance Transactions and the Balance of Payments*, Geneva Papers on Risk and Insurance

No. 6 (Geneva: Association Internationale pour l'Etude de l'Economie de l'Assurance, 1977).

GERARD M. DICKINSON and L.A. ROBERTS, *Capital Management in the UK General Insurance Companies* (London: Association of British Insurers, 1985).

GERARD M. DICKINSON and W. ZADJLIC, *Changing International Insurance Markets: their Implications for EEC Insurance Enterprises and Governments* (Brussels: Centre for European Policy Studies, 1986).

NEIL DOHERTY, *Insurance Pricing and Loss Prevention* (Farnborough, United Kingdom: Saxon House, 1976).

J. FINSINGER, E. HAMMOND and J. TAPP, *Insurance: Competition or Regulation* (London: Institute for Fiscal Studies, 1985).

MILTON FRIEDMAN, 'The Case for Flexible Exchange Rates', in R.E. Caves and H.G. Johnson (eds), *Readings in International Economics* (Homewood, Illinois: Richard D. Irwin, for the American Economic Association, 1968).

PAUL GOLDBERG and CHARLES P. KINDLEBERGER, 'Towards a GATT for Investment: a Proposal for Supervision of the International Corporation', *Law and Policy in International Business*, Washington, Vol. 2, 1970.

BRIAN GRIFFITHS, *Invisible Barriers to Invisible Trade* (London: Macmillan, for the Trade Policy Research Centre, 1975).

JOHN R. HICKS, *Essays in World Economics* (Oxford: Oxford University Press, 1957).

BRIAN HINDLEY, *Economic Analysis and Insurance Policy in the Third World* (London: Trade Policy Research Centre, 1982).

Freedom of Transport Insurance (Paris: International Chamber of Commerce, 1975).

HARRY G. JOHNSON, 'Optimal Trade Intervention in the Presence of Domestic Distortions', in Richard E. Caves *et al.*, *Trade Growth and the Balance of Payments* (Amsterdam: North Holland, 1965).

HARRY G. JOHNSON, *Comparative Costs and Commercial Policy: Theory for a Developing World Economy* (Stockholm: Almqvist & Wicksell, 1968).

RAYMOND J. KROMMENACKER, *Les Nations Unies et l'Assurance Reasssurance* (Paris: R. Pichon et R. Durand-Auzias, 1975).

RAYMOND J. KROMMENACKER, *The Liberalization of Investment Trade and the Inclusion of Services in GATT Negotiations: the Case of Transport Insurance* (Geneva: Association Internationale pour l'Étude de l'Economie de l'Assurance, 1976).

Liberalization of Trade in Services (LOTIS) (London: Committee on Invisible Exports, 1982).

H. LOUBERGE, *Reinsurance and the Foreign Exchange Risk*, Geneva Papers on Risk and Insurance No. 11 (Geneva: Association Internationale pour l'Étude de l'Economie de l'Assurance, 1979).

W.R. MALINOWSKI, 'European Insurance and the Third World', *Journal of World Trade Law*, London, August-September 1971.

SIR FRANK MCFADZEAN *et al.*, *Towards an Open World Economy*, Report of an Advisory Group (London: Macmillan, for the Trade Policy Research Centre, 1972).

J.A.S. NEAVE, 'Development of Government Involvement in Reinsurance Underwriting', in *Speaking of Reinsurance...* (Brentford, Middlesex: Kluwer Publishing, 1980).

J.A.S. NEAVE, 'The Effect on International Reinsurance of Changing Pattersn in Economic Relationships', in *Speaking of Reinsurance* ... (Brentford, Middlesex: Kluwer Publishing, 1980).

High Level Group on Trade and Related Problems, *Policy Perspectives for International Trade and Economic Relations*, Rey Report (Paris: OECD Secretariat, 1972).

International Investment and Multinational Enterprises (Paris: OECD Secretariat, 1976).

International Trade in Services: Insurance — Identification and Analysis of Obstacles (Paris: OECD Secretariat, 1983).

José Ripoll, 'UNCTAD and Insurance', *Journal of World Trade Law*, London, January-February 1974.

José Ripoll, 'Some Thoughts on Development and Insurance', *Best's Review*, Oldwick, New Jersey, February 1976.

José Ripoll 'Should the Barriers Come Down', *Best's Review*, Oldwick, New Jersey, November 1983.

David Robertson, 'Operations of Multinational Enterprises in Perspective', in Hugh Corbet and Robert Jackson (eds), *In Search of a New World Economic Order* (London: Croom Helm, for the Trade Policy Research Centre, 1974).

J.J. Rosa, 'Les economies des dimensions des institutions financieres', *Banque*, Paris, May 1972.

Ronald K. Shelp, 'The Proliferation of Foreign Insurance Laws: Reform on Regression', *Law and Policy in International Business*, No. 8, 1976.

Ronald K. Shelp, *Beyond Industrialization: Ascendancy of the Global Service Economy* (New York: Praeger, 1981).

Harold D. Skipper, 'Protectionism in the Provision of International Insurance Services', *Journal of Risk and Insurance*, Orlando, Vol. LIV, No. 1, 1987.

Bo Södersten, *International Economics* (London: Macmillan, 1974).

ROBERT M. STERN, *The Balance of Payments* (London: Macmillan, 1974).

PAUL STREETEN and FRANCES STEWART, 'Conflict Between Output and Employment Objectives in Developing Countries', in Paul Streeten (ed.), *Frontiers of Development Studies* (London: Macmillan, 1972).

List of Thames Essays

OCCASIONAL papers of the Trade Policy Research Centre are published under the omnibus heading of Thames Essays. Set out below are the particulars of those published to date. The first 54 titles may be obtained from the Centre. Titles 55 onwards are available from the publishers, Harvester Wheatsheaf.

1 GERARD and VICTORIA CURZON, *Hidden Barriers to International Trade* (1970), 75 pp.

2 T.E. JOSLING, *Agriculture and Britain's Trade Policy Dilemma* (1970), 52 pp.

3 GERARD and VICTORIA CURZON, *Global Assault on Non-tariff Trade Barriers* (1972), 44 pp.

4 BRIAN HINDLEY, *Britain's Position on Non-tariff Protection* (1972), 60 pp.

5 GEOFFREY DENTON and SEAMUS O'CLEIREACAIN, *Subsidy Issues in International Commerce* (1972), 75 pp.

6 GEORGE F. RAY, *Western Europe and the Energy Crisis* (1975), 68 pp.

7 THEODORE GEIGER, JOHN VOLPE and ERNEST H. PREEG, *North American Integration and Economic Blocs* (1975), 65 pp.

8 HUGH CORBET, W.M. CORDEN, BRIAN HINDLEY, ROY BATCHELOR and PATRICK MINFORD, *On How to Cope with Britain's Trade Position* (1977), 80 pp.

50 ROBERT E. HUDEC, *Developing Countries in the GATT Legal System* (1988), 255 pp.

51 DEEPAK LAL and SARATH RAJAPATIRANA, *Impediments to Trade Liberalization in Sri Lanka* (1989), 94 pp.

52 JIMMYE S. HILLMAN and ROBERT A. ROTHENBERG, *Agricultural Trade and Protection in Japan* (1988), 96 pp.

53 J.P. HAYES, *Economic Effects of Sanctions on Southern Africa* (1987), 100 pp.

54 ROMEO M. BAUTISTA, *Impediments to Trade Liberalization in the Philippines* (1989), 90 pp.

55 KYM ANDERSON and RODNEY TYERS, *Global Effects of Liberalizing Trade in Farm Products* (1991), 120 pp.

56 RODNEY DE C. GREY, *Concepts of Trade Diplomacy and Trade in Services* (1991), 208 pp.

57 ROBERT L. CARTER and GERARD M. DICKINSON, *Obstacles to the Liberalization of Trade in Insurance* (1991), 208 pp.